AF540575

SAILING

DPH SPORTS SERIES

SAILING

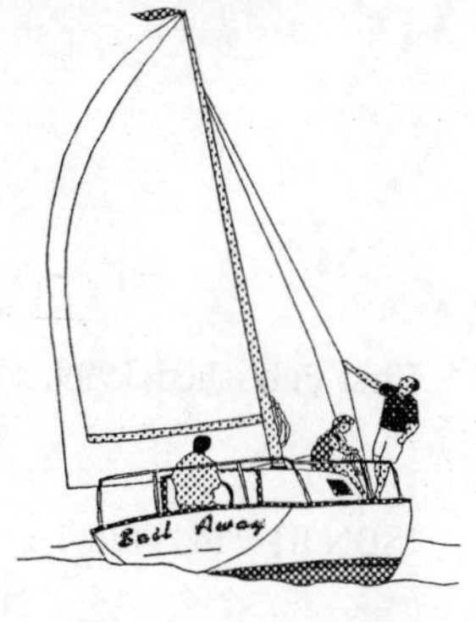

Ashok Kumar

1999
DISCOVERY PUBLISHING HOUSE
New Delhi-110002

First Published-1999

ISBN 81-7141-476-1

Published by:
DISCOVERY PUBLISHING HOUSE
4831/24, Ansari Road, Prahlad Street,
Daryaganj, New Delhi-110 002 (*INDIA*)
Phone: 3279245
Fax: 91-11-3253475

Printed at:

ARORA OFFSET PRESS
Laxmi Nagar, Delhi-92

PREFACE

The need of having a sports series felt because today's situation of the world is not conducive to peace, all round there is destruction, despair, conflict and war; war if not between two nations then within the country itself. In a world where there are some 820 million people unemployed or under-employed, and where 86 million people are born every year, it is not surprising that one out of every four individuals lives in absolute poverty. The *Discovery Publishing House* by Publishing this series seeks to get positive response as—to means by which sports can promote and propagate peace and international cooperation. Sportsmen form a large identifiable cadre. We visualises a situation where a conscious efforts is made all over the world to train the sportspersons to spread the message of peace and international cooperation. Instead of peace keeping efforts through arms and army, the sportspersons may be used as soldiers of peace in a subtle manner. The effort is to make the realize the contribution of sports as a factor for sustainable development, peace keeping and international cooperation.

In developing countries, sports development cooperation is still in the need of justification and steadfast arguments. Many people ask the question "why invest in sports in developing countries for which water supply, health service and agriculture projects are much better suited? An apt reply to this question may be "for many of the people of a developing country,

Sports is the only 'Sweaty' Leisure-time activity. Sports represents a moment of joy in the midst of hard poverty-stricken and dirty everyday life. Doing sports even makes one's work go more smoothly the next day.

This series will be useful to the sports promoters, organisers, coaches and other persons related or interested in sports.

Editor

CONTENTS

CONTENTS

1

SAFETY

The reader should study the whole chapter and begin to prepare equipment, practice techniques, and adopt safe habits. A Bronze Sail student will have to demonstrate safe habits as a normal procedure. It takes time and experience to develop sensible judgement about how to avoid dangerous situations. A skipper is responsible for the safety of his crew and guests. An untrained person on board cannot be expected to react correctly to every new or emergency situation. Know their limitations and train or brief them before committing them to potential danger. Sailing is a relatively safe sport and recreation, despite conditions that are often unpredictable. The reason is that modern equipment, clothing and techniques, developed from research and experience, protect sailors when properly used, Wearing a lifejacket or PFD is now both comfortable and accepted. 'The problems we must avoid or cope with are: capsize, cold water hypothermia, risk of drowning, failing overboard, collision, fire, being blown out to sea or on to a rocky shore. We may even be concerned about being becalmed with sail power, being exhausted, uncomfortable or just losing one's position in a race by capsize. Enjoyment is the name of the game and without safety, it is gone.

Safe for sailing

There are many questions to ask oneself before going

sailing. Some are not obvious without previous experience. You must be prepared for unseen changes or wait for better conditions. Here are some of the questions to be considered in order to make sensible decisions: Can you interpret weather signs and forecasts? Are there local sailing hazards? Is air or water temperature cold? What strength and direction of wind is expected? Are waves likely to increase in size? Are boats to be used suitable and safe? What skill has both skipper and crew? What supervision and rescue facilities are available?

Suppose on a warm summer evening in June, two young sailors decided to go sailing. They had both earned their White

Sail Level III. Wind was from the west along the shore at about 10 knots and waves quite small.

When deciding to go sailing in these good conditions, the following was not taken into consideration:

1) Posted Club weather forecast said, "Winds light, shifting to strong North Westerly in the evening and cooler." They failed to read it.

2) Although the air was warm, the water in this lake is always cold in June because it is large and deep. They were not dressed for it.

3) They were PFD's but no warm clothing or wet suits, Capsize and cold water was not considered.

4) They did not inform the safety officer or anyone of their intention to go sailing.

5) The boat used was a small 12 ft. dinghy not easily self-rescued.

6) It was only 2 hours from normal sundown.

The following events could easily have occurred and led to a disaster:

1) When only a quarter of a mile out from the harbour, the wind veered to the N.W, and gusted to 25 knots.

2) It clouded over and became colder. It would soon be dark and wind was now offshore, open water downwind, They headed for shore.

3) Returning to harbour or shore was now a beat, progress was slow due to increasing waves and gusts.

4) They might have made it on their own, but the tiller broke and then with makeshift tiller they capsized,

5) The boat soon went mast down, the centreboard dropped into the hull out of reach and self-rescue was nearly impossible. They soon felt cold and weak.

6) They were now completely dependent on someone seeing them who would be able to help before dark and before they became helpless in the cold water.

7) Let us assume they were lucky. Another boat saw them and got them ashore in time before Hypothermia was too serious. Once it gets dark, even when warmly dressed, the risk of exposure and possible death is greater. If you can self-rescue and keep warm, you must still be lucky in that someone sees your plight if anything goes wrong.

This example illustrates that not being prepared for any possible problem may cause great risk. The decision should have been made not to go out of the harbour when forecast conditions were not within their capabilities in the boat used. These sailors learned a lesson they will never forget. They assisted the safety officer in developing dinghy safety rules for their club.

Self-rescue techniques were learned, boat equipment was improved and experience was passed on to others.

The following points should be observed to avoid potentially dangerous situations:

1) Dress suitably for cold in case of capsize, A wet suit or thermal float jacket is recommended for below 10°C water.

2) Get permission from sailing instructor or safety officer for use of club boats. Observe club rules and small craft warnings.

3) Be sure rescue craft are within sight.

a) Conditions to consider

1) Weather affects visibility and water temperature. Strong winds cause capsize and waves, Direction of wind affects potential waves in sailing area or harbour entrance. The stronger 'It blows, and the longer the stretch of water, the higher waves can build. The longer the time it blows, the larger the waves will be.

2) Newspaper weather forecasts, club weather bulletins, radio weather reports, marine forecasts, storm warnings, weather signs and predicted changes should be considered and interpreted into potential hazards in that location.

3) Consider if the wind or waves create a danger of running ashore on rocks or being blown out to sea if disabled or capsized.

4) Will evening come before your return without running lights, make rescue impossible, or navigation of hazards difficult?

5) Consider cold water as the major danger if you fall into the water.

6) Are tide, current or hidden rocks potential hazards?

b) Safety equipment

1) Is your boat capable of Self-rescue when capsized? Have you tried it in actual conditions with your crew?

2) Do you wear a life jacket or P.F.D. most of the time? If you fall overboard, it may be too late even if stowed in the boat.

3) If water is below 10°C, wet suitor floater jacket should be mandatory depending on degree of supervision available.

4) Do you have M.O.T. required equipment for your type of craft such as 2 paddles, bailer, lights, plus painter for towing. See Boating Safety Guide.

c) Self-rescue ability

1) If a capsize occurs will you need help to get the boat righted and sail back in any possible condition?

2) Are your crew and guests briefed or capable of Self-rescue in the particular boat?

3) If you fall overboard as skipper or crew is someone capable of picking you up?

4) If capsized and not Sure you can right the boat, how long can you last considering clothing and water temperature.

5) Are you a skilled enough sailor for the possible conditions?

6) Is your physical condition equal to the tiring

procedures of righting a poorly-equipped boat, especially when cold.

d) Club safety checks

1) Do you have permission from the sailing instructor to use club boats in the conditions expected?
2) Is there a safety check-out system or someone to whom you can report your departure and return?
3) Are there enough rescue boats for the sailing instruction class or the number of boats racing if a storm strikes.
4) Do beginners in sailing class have basic training in capsize and emergency procedure in case of need?
5) If water is cold and no rescue boats are available, do you use the buddy system to assure help is available?

Clothing for sailing

To enjoy sailing we should be comfortable. To be safe while sailing, we must avoid the risk to hypothermia (exposure to cold and dangerous loss of inner body heat). What we wear to suit conditions is very important.

Conditions in the sailing season in most parts of Canada can vary from very cool and windy, to raining, or hot and sunny. Water temperatures also vary greatly with not only the season but the body of water and previous direction of the wind across that water. In summer, the warm surface water is blown across the surface of a large lake by an offshore breeze and is replaced by 6°C water from below. If wind is blowing onshore for a few hours or days, depending on size of the lake, the water will be comfortably warm. The dangerous cold water months are May and June.

Clothing for sailing must be practical, comfortable and suited to changing conditions. The following points should be helpful in selecting suitable clothing:

Shoes should be canvas top, easily dried when wet with nonslip rubber soles. A herring bone pattern sole that squeezes the water from wet slippery surfaces will give a safe grip. It is not advisable to sail on any kind of boat without shoes. There is always danger of cuts while wading during launching, hurting toes while sailing or slipping on wet fiberglass or painted surfaces. Shoes also protect feet from cuts on self-bailers while self-rescuing.

Socks should be worn for comfort and warmth if water is cool. Heavy woollen socks, even when wet, have an insulating effect. When cool weather sailing, some sailors like to wear specially designed thermal boots that keep the feet warm and dry if you don't have to wade out from shore. Short rubber boots with nonslip soles are popular for keeping feet dry, but m a capsize they make swimming very difficult.

Pants. There are various preferences on this subject. Some prefer shorts in hot weather, or even in cool weather, so the skin will dry off after spray much faster than trousers or jeans. It the water is very cold, however, wearing shorts is a dangerous practice because there is very little protection against hypothermia in the water. You may need protection against sunburn, cold wind, cold water or the cooling effect of evaporation by wind on wet clothing. Storm wear pants, loose fitting over trousers or slacks, and long underwear, are an economical partial substitute for wet suit in cold water. There should be heavy duty elastic shoulder straps to allow for active bending and hiking. Lightweight rubberized nylon will not stand up for long and good quality pays in the long run.

Wet Suit. Maximum full-length protection can be obtained with 1/8 thick nitrogen-blown neoprene foam rubber. Stretch nylon on both sides improves strength and flexibility. Zippers in arms and legs and full length at the front, plus nylon lining, make it easier to put on. Some are made overlapping, two-piece and should be form-fitting. They prevent loss of heat from critical areas even without full legs or arms. Although wet inside, it feels warm and reasonably comfortable except in hot weather. To prevent wear and tear, clothing can be worn over a wet suit as well as a PFD. It does not take the place of a PFD.

Sweaters. The top of the body can be kept warm for some time in cold water with heavy wool sweaters and storm wear, They soak up a lot of water which can weigh up to 40 extra pounds when trying to get out of the water. Wear a turtleneck sweater to prevent cold water going down the neck. Even a small towel will help here.

Storm Wear—Rain and Wind Proof. This is available in a variety of designs, materials and colours. A bright colour is best, orange or yellow for visibility. Non-rotting nylon fabric is preferable inside because they always condense and trap moisture inside in cold wind from perspiration. Some have front zippers oı may be pullover style. Hoods are usually provided and prevent water going down the neck. Quality material will last many times longer for the cost, also stitching, zippers and drawstrings are better. They are also popular in full length suits for crews in wet racing boats. If 2 piece, be sure the pants come up high and the jacket is long to prevent waves penetrating.

Floater Jacket. This is a practical solution to the problems of keeping warm, dry, comfortable and safer if you fall overboard. They are M.O.T. approved in orange colour and the U-VIC one designed by the University of Victoria has many features added. A foam rubber fold-down flap can be passed between the legs and clipped at the front to form pants. It has a neckband, hood and radar reflector panel. It has the ability to float a person face up. In the heat escape lessening posture when knees are drawn up and ankles crossed, some contact with the boat or another person will assure stability. It can also be worn with zipper open and does not condense moisture on the inside surface. A good floater jacket costs no more than a good P.F.D. and storm jacket. It is handier and more comfortable than a wet suit, but cannot protect the legs.

Hats. Sunburn is common to many sailors at the beginning of the season and to fair-skinned persons, all season, In summer a lightweight hat with brim all around or peak to protect the forehead is commonly worn. When the sun is hazy, burning occurs in half the time because sun reflects from all directions and from the water. The worst danger in sun is sunstroke,

One problem in windy weather, especially when racing, is keeping a hat on, A skipper with both hands busy needs a hat with elastic headband or elastic chinstrap. In cool weather, a wool or nylon knitted toque is warm and stays on well. Keeping the head warm is a big factor in extending survival time in cold water.

Sun glasses are advisable while sailing in bright or hazy sun. They filter out ultraviolet rays that penetrate the skin even around the eyes which may cause sore or tired eyes or headaches. Fair-skinned people must use sun screen or hat and sun glasses most of the time on the water. A polaroid lens is ideal because it filters out vertical rays that reflect off shiny surfaces like water and shows up patches of wind, gusts or cat's paws as they appear on the water to windward. They can be clipped on glasses to save buying prescription sun glasses. It pays to clip a lanyard to glasses because they sink very fast if knocked into the water.

Keel boat Procedures

In a keelboat, which many dinghy sailors will sail aboard sooner or later, manoverboard is the greatest danger. It poses different problems and procedures. "One hand for yourself and one for the ship" is good advice on deck or in the cockpit. The first action is to throw a life ring or jacket to him immediately. Appoint someone aboard to watch him in the water constantly. Begin to count the seconds you sail away. Bear off to a beam reach immediately and gybe to be able to return in the shortest time. Sighting the victim is easier at right angles to the wave direction, but in a minute you could be 200 yards or meters away, so return quickly and safely using experience of prior practice, When returning, luff Up Slowly, stopping just to windward of the person on your lee bow in a keel boat. The boat will not capsize, and the deck being lower it is easier to get aboard. Have a heaving line and boat hook ready. Put a line Linder his arms and either heave to or drop the jib if he cannot get aboard. Getting a heavy person aboard will depend on their heavy wet clothing, weight, exhaustion or condition in cold water. Put a line around him under the arms. If he is able to use it, provide a stepping assist with a bowline loop lowered to his foot, adjusted and cleated. You may have to lower the mainsail and use main halyard and winch to get him aboard. Do not get in the water to help. The rule in windy weather should be lifejackets when on deck. When seas are running, lifelines and safety harness also should be mandatory. At night, both are required by all sensible skippers. Lifejackets should be equipped with a light. Those who race keelboats have very strict and sensible rules for safety. They use a manoverboard marker which is lit at night. The most difficult problem is to keep the person in sight in waves or find them again if lost.

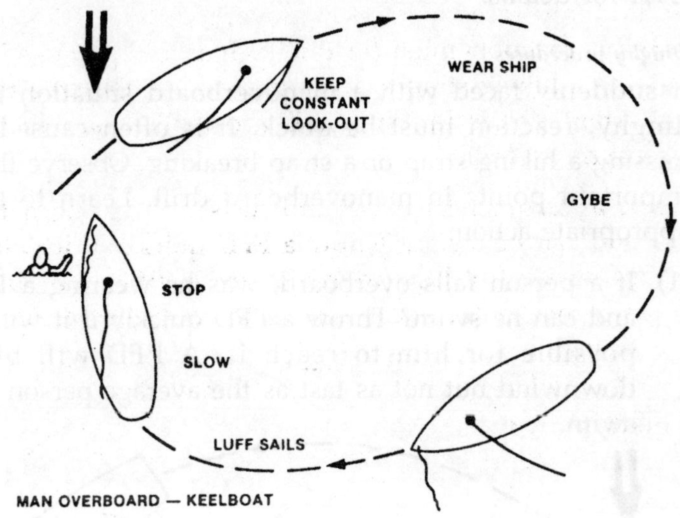

Fig. 1

Perhaps the most important point to remember as a skipper is never invite persons on board in poor conditions unless there is someone aboard who can recover you if you fall overboard. This means that manoverboard practice by your crew even with a buoy is very important safety procedure. The second point is that hypothermia is the greatest danger in cold water when serious trouble arises. Insist that children wear lifejackets on deck at all times. They are the most vulnerable to cold water exposure.

CYA Cruising Standards are now widely used and are taught and tested at sailing schools by CYA certified instructors across the country. They cover a great many safety procedures for cruising skippers and crews. Everyone sailing a keelboat should earn the Basic Coastal Cruising level certificate at least. The Advanced Coastal Cruising course is the next level of proficiency. Write CYA for details.

Dinghy procedures

If suddenly faced with a manoverboard situation in a dinghy, reaction must be quick. It is often caused by missing a hiking strap or a strap breaking. Observe these important points in manoverboard drill. Learn to take appropriate action:

(1) If a person falls overboard, was he wearing a PFD and can he swim? Throw a PFD quickly if it will be possible for him to reach it. A PFD will blow downwind but not as fast as the average person can swim.

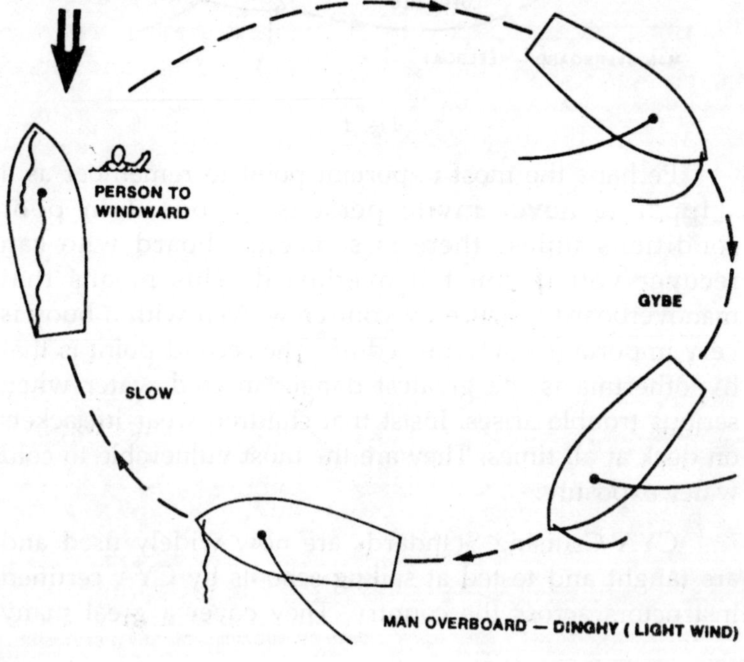

Fig. 2

(2) Note the location of the person in the water in relation to the shore and especially in relation to the wind direction. In a sea, the hardest problem if you sail on too far, is to find the person again if lost from sight. Steer in a direction across the wind, turn and return on a reach so that you can luff sails as necessary to control speed and heeling. Beating back upwind alone is more difficult and running is more dangerous in a heavy wind. Try to locate the person at all times by relating your position upwind or downwind and approximate boat lengths across the wind from where he fell overboard.

(3) Decide whether to gybe or tack to return as soon as possible. If winds up to 10 mph, gybing is safe and faster, but in heavier winds tacking is safer than a gybe due to its greater risk of capsize if not done properly. When alone in the boat, tacking must be done properly to avoid getting into irons. Drop the centreboard all the way, head up to a beat and when reasonable speed is attained, tack quickly between waves and do not lose your balance.

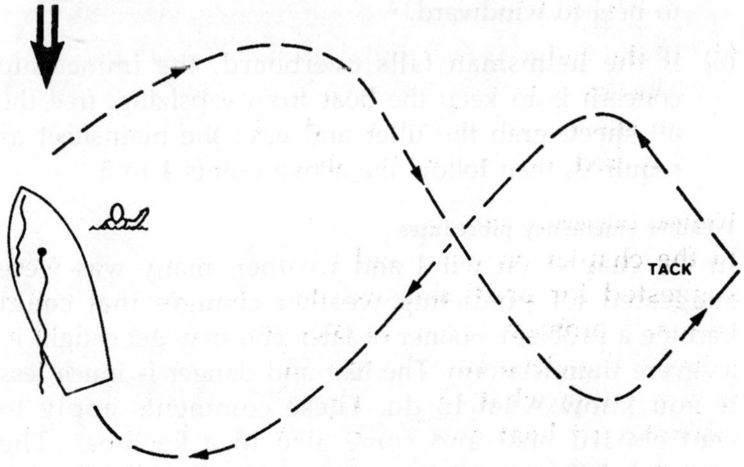

MAN OVERBOARD — DINGHY (HEAVY WIND)

Fig. 3

(4) Return on a reach, steering slightly downwind of the person in the water and head up slowly. Luff sails as if to pick up a mooring in order to stop on the lee side of the person. If you stop to windward in a dinghy there is greater risk of capsizing when pulling the person aboard or of waves pushing the boat on him. Have a line ready to throw in case you just miss the first time. Grasp a wrist, let go of the tiller and move to a fore-and-aft position near the shrouds to keep the boat from turning into the wind or bearing away. The drag of the person in the water will act as a sea anchor. Practice is necessary in a particular boat to develop a feel for stopping and controlling the boat during rescue. Be sure to have your crew practise the drill also in case you are the man overboard.

(5) Getting the person aboard is the next problem. If he is heavy or tired and cold, it will take all his remaining strength and your coordinated assistance to get hims aboard. In a dinghy make a trial attempt to assess his condition and the tendency of the boat to heel to windward.

(6) If the helmsman falls overboard, the immediate concern is to keep the boat from capsizing, free the jib sheet, grab the tiller and ease the mainsheet as required, then follow the above points 1 to 5.

Weather emergency procedures

In the chapter on wind and weather, many was were suggested for predicting weather changes that could become a problem. Sooner or later you may get caught in a severe thunderstorm. The fear and danger is much less if you know what to do. These comments apply to centreboard boat and some also to a keelboat. The essential difference is the greater danger in a keelboat if you run aground and the smaller danger of swamping or capsizing. Waves are often the worst problem in a storm especially near shore.

Waves

Wind causes waves to develop according to fairly predictable rules. This is useful information for mental calculation of potential danger in storms in various locations. Some wave data, useful in predictions and boat handling are as follows:

(1) Wave height is from crest to trough.

(2) Wave length is from crest to crest or trough to trough.

(3) Waves generally move in the same direction as the median wind.

(4) Very little water actually moves except for a surface flow on each wave. The wave itself travels along carrying its energy with it like a wave travelling along a rope. Water moves up the top half of the back of a wave, along the top, and half way down the front or other side. In the trough it is moving against the direction of the wave.

(5) Wave height increases rapidly with wind speed increase.

(6) Wave height increases rapidly during the first 6 hours the wind is blowing.

(7) The "fetch" or distance the wind sweeps increases wave height and wave length.

(8) The period of a wave is the time in seconds for two successive crests to pass one point. It allows easy calculation of wave speed.

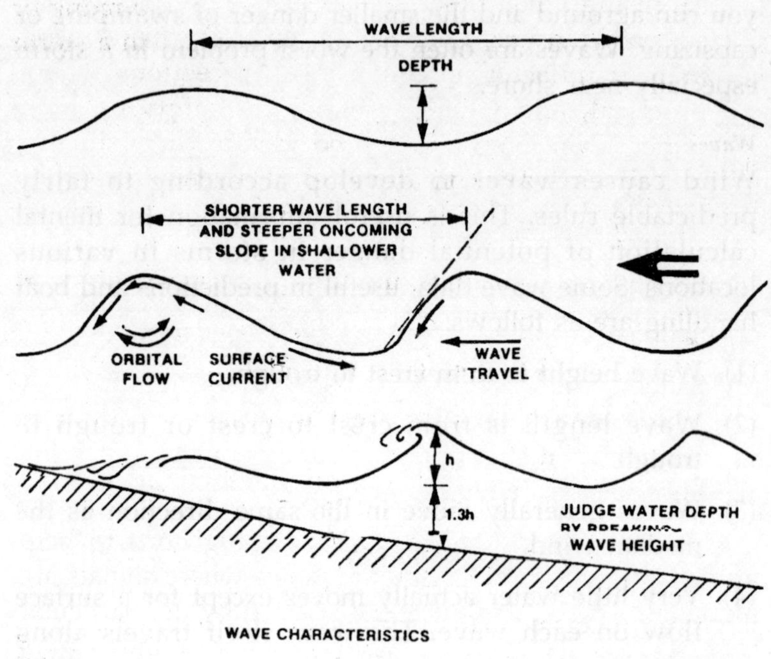

Fig. 4

Fog

This is a weather emergency that can descend without much warning. Fortunately fog is less likely when there is much wind and wave. These are a few helpful suggestions to avoid the two worst problems, collision and getting lost:

Collision

(1) Collision is a real danger in busy channels or shipping lanes. The best means to avoid collision is by both using universal fog signal and by listening for others. Most boats do not have radar equipment, but at least every boat should have radar reflectors. A mast, when made of aluminum and not heeled will be picked up on a radar screen. It can be very

confusing when other signals also show on a radar screen. Transport Canada call for a 10 square meter area of reflector, effective in all directions where practical, and where essential for safety on boat under 12 m long. It is a good idea to carry suitable reflective material on board for emergencies in fog.

Fog signals. See Government regulations.

(1) Sailboat on starboard gives 1 blast per minute.

(2) Sailboat on port tack gives 2 blasts per minute.

(3) Sailboa reach or run wind abaft the beam 3 blasts. A whistle, as used on lifejackets or an air horn, is useful on, small boat. A harbour entrance may have a fog horn to help guide boats.

A harbour entrance may have a fog horn to help guide boats back in fog. A chart shows where signals are located and how to identify the location by the particular sound. It is difficult to tell exactly where a sound is from or how far because transmission of sound varies with tone and weather, and density of fog.

Sound signals should be used, but they cannot be relied upon completely nor can radar, so consider fog as a danger to avoid if at all possible. Be on constant alert and try to keep track of where you are at all times before fog closes in.

Lost in fog

Without a compass it is very easy to get lost in fog or to atleast lose track of where you are, If you do not know your position on a chart, even a compass will not guide you because it is not possible to plot a course to your destination. If you normally sail only within sight of land and fog appears you must know: (a) where you are, (b) the compass direction You Move, (c) at what speed, (d) and for how long, Even this type of simple navigation is not very practical in a dinghy so you have only two choices: (1) anchor and wait if you have sound signals or (2) set a compass course for home before visibility is too poor to see shore.

Fog is like sailing at night when the sky is overcast and there are no shore lights visible. The only hope without a compass is to set a course and hope the wind does not change. This will not be accurate even if the weather system indicates steady wind direction. If you must go upwind and tack it becomes even more difficult and more dangerous when near shore. Often there is no wind at all in fog to depend on.

If you know your position and you have a chart and instruments to plot the direction and distance, you would have to use dead reckoning navigation to determine when you are close to a point near shore. You must measure the distance travelled through the water with a patent log while steering a plotted compass course. If current is present, it becomes more difficult to be accurate because you must estimate the current direction and speed at different locations to plot a course. A dinghy is not equipped for such navigation, so visual landmarks, use of soundings and a chart are helpful. If you know the area, checking the depth in fog or darkness may be the only means of safe return. The sound of waves on shore may also give a clue to your location, but it is much safer to avoid the situation if possible.

Motorboat rescue of a dinghy

A sailor should be aware of the best procedures for rescue of a sailboat and if necessary ask for specific help. An instructor must know the right approach under a variety of conditions, but a nonsailor, although willing to help, may need some guidance, The main thing to remember is that the safety of the people must come ahead of the rescue of the boat, In a sudden storm, rescue-motorboats must also consider the overall picture of the area and rescue people from several boats at a time, and, if necessary, leave other boats until later.

Equipment

The motorboat should be wide enough to be seaworthy. A rubber duck or inflatable outboard is low and does not cause injury or damage. A Boston whaler is popular as a rescue boat because it is stable and roomy. The following should be carried in the rescue boat:

— Oars or 2 paddles. Oars are better if the motor fails.

— Spare PFDs or floater coat.

— Danforth Anchor and 100 ft of 1/4" nylon line.

— 60 ft of nylon tow rope 5/16" diameter.

— 2 two-gallon bailing buckets.

— First aid kit.

— Fire extinguisher.

Optional equipment useful in some cases:

— Loud hailer or megaphone, flares, marker, buoy, boat hook, Spare gasoline, blanket, hot drink.

People—Identify the condition and needs of the sailors.

(1) Approach cautiously from downwind. Avoid injury from propeller. Put in neutral.

(2) Find out if anyone is drowning, unconscious or injured.

(3) Identify physical condition and protection of sailors in cold water.

(4) Find out if help is needed. Open hand—yes. Closed fist—no. Sailors racing may be wishing to continue when righted and need some assistance. Stand-by if possible.

(5) Find out if the sailors are exhausted or capable of helping right the boat. If exhausted take them aboard.

(6) Ask what assistance they require. It may be only necessary to tow the boat into the wind to right it. They may need help to get the boat on its side from the turtled position. They may need treatment for hypothermia first, Sailors tend to overestimate their self-rescue ability when cold or exhausted.

The sailboat

Identify if the crew must be taken ashore first or the boat righted and towed back to shore with crew. Is the boat turtled, on its side or upright and swamped? Are the crew capable of sailing back after assistance in righting? When the type of rescue required is established, proceed as follows:

(a) *If the boat is on its side:*

(1) Tow the boat into the wind to prevent recapsize.

(2) Find out if the mast is full of water and too heavy. If so, go to the tip of the mast and help raise it.

(3) When centreboard can be used to lever it up, keep the bow head-to-wind until either the crew can right the boat and empty the water, or until they are ready to sail it dry using transom scuppers.

(4) If the boat is swamped and there is not enough buoyancy to bail it, lower sails. Take crew on board the motorboat or at least out of the sailboat, lift the

bow to dump water out of the stern, then have someone bail the rest.

(5) If the boat is to be towed, get the sails down and stowed before towing. Have someone sit in the boat and steer if possible with centreboard one quarter down. Tie the tow rope around the mast if there is any doubt about the painter or bow fitting strength.

(6) If the boat has too little buoyancy when on its side, have the weight of only one person on it when righting, or raise the mast by working up the shroud. Save time bailing by letting it float higher before righting.

(b) *If the boat is turtled:*

This makes rescue difficult, especially if the crew have been unsuccessful because of location of buoyancy to right it. If the centreboard has dropped into the hull, proceed as follows from the motorboat:

(1) Approach the sailboat on the lee side, pull along side, and slowly pull up on the gunwale. Gradually work your hands up the shroud as the boat moves farther away until you reach the tip of the mast. Raise the mast over your head and work back down the mast and the other shroud until the boat rights itself. Be sure the bow is facing into the wind.

(2) If the mast is at an angle to the water, it may be stuck in the mud or sand. The waves tend to push it in further. Tie a tow rope to the mast and tow from over the hull's gunwale in the opposite direction to the way it went in. If it is pointing down very steeply, pull from under the hull with short line but steadily and not enough to bend the mast. It might even pay to dive down in clear water to see the problem then decide how best to proceed.

Rescue techniques

(1) Do not risk damage to the boat by getting too close in waves. The danger always exists that a motor left idling for too long, while observing or manoeuvring, could stop when spark plugs get fouled and not restart. Oars are better for holding a boat in position than paddles, but neither are any help for towing. It is possible for a motorboat to help get a sailboat upright, then be towed ashore by the sailboat.

(2) Observe the possible dangers downwind from rocks, weeds or shoals. If you must leave a boat floating it is wise to anchor it if the depth allows. You can set the anchor with the motorboat and allow enough scope and fasten to the bow or painter.

(3) Avoid getting the propeller tangled in sheets or line from the sailboat. Put the shift in neutral when close, or shut off the motor.

(4) To tow a boat's bow into the wind it is safer when waves are not too high to go bow to bow to keep the propeller away from the crew when in the water. In waves, the crew in the water must fasten the painter to a tow line securely using a double sheet bend.

Towing

A knowledge of towing techniques is required by both the towboat and sailboat crew. In sailing schools and after race: when the wind drops, often a large group of boats must be towed by a small motorboat. This is possible in smooth water if the towline is long enough and the speed is kept low, Friction varies as the square of the speed, so towing fast puts great loads on boats, lines and motor.

In rough waters usually only a single boat can be

towed, but great forces occur if towing is not planned properly.

Towing a group of boats: If only a few boats are being towed, they can be towed in line, but remember all the friction force is carried on the first boat and its painter. It is better to split up half on each side of the motorboat transom. More boats requires a heavy towline with each boat tied to it using a rolling hitch. Follow these rules for towing:

(1) If you need a tow, have sails down and stowed.

(2) Hold up a coil of towline to signify you need a tow.

(3) Be ready to heave a line to the towboat. Be sure you have your end fastened to the mast or painter where it is strong enough to take the full load.

(4) Raise centreboard if towing in-line, leaving only enough board for steerage or to keep the two lines of boats apart.

(5) Use a rolling hitch with slip hitch to fasten your painter or two lines to the central tow line.

(6) Sit a little aft while steering to keep the bow from burying but avoid stern drag too.

(7) When towing boats behind in line, tie the next boat's line or painter to your thwart by 2 or 3 turns around and a slip hitch or just hold tension on it. Do not use transom track or cleats or even thwart if you are not sure it can take the strain of all boats behind.

Towing a single boat in waves and smooth water

Forces on towlines can be very great in waves when the boat being towed is going up a wave and the tow boat is going down trying to accelerate. Lines must be strong and not capable of too much stretch like an anchor rope.

The distance between the centre of each boat must be the same as, or a multiple of, the distance between waves or wavelength. Both boats must go up each wave, or accelerate down each wave at the same time. The pattern is sometimes broken so the line must be capable of withstanding periodic stress greater than normal.

In smooth water, a dinghy tow line must be adjusted in length to suit the stern wave of a planing motor boat. The lines should keep the bow just ahead of the crest of the wave to keep drag to a minimum. The sailboat must be at least level and the motor boat should maintain a steady speed to keep the stern wave at the same distance behind it. If the stern wave is too close, lengthen the tow rope and keep the bow from nosing into the wave. Always steer towards the point your line is fastened to when being towed.

Warnings

(1) Never tow a capsized sailboat.

(2) Never tow a boat full of water.

(3) Never tow too fast. A capsize would sheer off the rigging.

(4) Always keep a lookout for the towed boat.

(5) Some small sailboats will fill with water through the centreboard trunk if towed too fast.

(6) Always be ready to cast off a towline when getting near a dock.

(7) Be ready to anchor in case a current is flowing and the motor stops.

2

THEORY OF SAILING

One of the keys to expert sailing is an understanding of sailing theory. What makes a boat go faster or slower, why it heels so much, and why it capsizes can best be studied using lines called Vectors. A Vector looks like an arrow that shows direction, but it is drawn so that its length represents quantity. Vectors can represent graphically the speed of the wind, of a boat or a current. They may also show how sail forces act and how resisting forces help to keep a boat in weight and turning balance.

In sailing, vectors can be used to study two separate phenomena force and velocity. They are unrelated. Velocity vectors will be studied first to show how the wind on a moving boat actually affects the sails. Vectors can also be used to plot a boat's' course sailing in a current to find out how fast it will travel and in what direction.

Velocity vectors

Velocity vectors are drawn to scale in the direction they act Each one is drawn to a convenient scale to represent a rate of speed of wind, boat or current in nautical miles per hour (Knots) (K) or Kilometers per hr. km/h. When we combine the effect of the wind created by the movement of the boat and the true wind, we can represent the apparent wind on the boat by a resultant vector. We can also determine what direction to steer in a current to reach a destination by representing boat speed and direction by a vector and current speed and direction over the ground by another vector. When these are added we can measure the true speed and course made good by a vector diagram.

The following factors are noted:

1. A direction arrow E is not drawn to scale and is not a vector.
2. A velocity vector drawn to a scale represents rate of speed. For example, if 10 knots speed is represented by a vector 1 cm long the scale is 10 knots = 1 cm and a line 2.5 cm long represents 25 Knots. Velocity = Vector length x scale.
3. 1 nautical mile per hour (1 Knot) = 1.1 mph (approx.)
   1 Knot (1 K) 1.85 km/h
   1 km = .6214 (about 5/8) statute miles
   1 km/h = .6214 mph
4. A compass bearing is a direction arrow measured in degrees clockwise from North. North East is a bearing of 45°.

Vector addition

In sailing theory, the effect of one wind on another ora current on a boat's course can be resolved graphically.

The method to be used is called vector addition. It works for any sailing vector problem if we can first identify the components to be added and which is the resultant effect. Two component vectors added by vector addition equals one resultant vector.

If two velocity vectors act from a point, the resultant vector will also act from the same point.

Example of vector addition

The first vector component is 4 units long acting North, the 2nd is 7 units long acting East from point B. Add the vectors and find the resultant vector length and direction.

Steps

1) Draw a Vector AB 4 units long north.

2) Draw a 2nd Vector from B, 7 units long east. (BC)

3) To find the resultant join AC and measure it to the same scale of units used to draw AB & BC. The resultant acting from A is equivalent to AB & BC and measures 8.5 units long. ABC is the velocity vector triangle.

It does not matter in which order the 4 & 7 unit components are added. Draw AD then DC and join AC. The resultant AC is the same and triangle ABC & ADC are the same shape and size.

ABCD forms a parallelogram because opposite sides are equal and parallel. This shape is useful when resolving a resultant into 2 components. Note that AB and AD are also components of the resultant AC because they are equal to DC & BC, respectively.

Apparent wind

Apparent Wind is the wind felt by a boat that is moving. If the boat is stopped it feels only true wind. If there is no wind and a boat is driven forward under power, the apparent wind will come from dead ahead at the same speed as the boat is moving. A flag on the boat will blow aft because the wind is blowing aft relative to the boat. This wind will be called "Boat Wind".

This is a simple method to find apparent wind speed and direction no matter what the heading or direction of true wind. From the mast, draw a boat wind velocity vector to the same scale you would choose for a "true wind" vector. It will be the same velocity as boat speed but acting towards the stern as boat wind does. To find the effect of true wind on boat wind, add a true wind vector by vector addition, meeting the boat wind vector at the mast. Draw the resultant to join the 2 vectors and measure the velocity (speed and direction) of the apparent wind on that resultant. The angle of the apparent wind will always be forward of the "true wind" angle. If you wish to show apparent wind meeting at the mast simply draw "Boat Wind" to meet at the mast and true wind to meet at the tail of "boat wind". Again, vector addition will give the correct resultant.

Try an example of a boat reaching at 5 knots North. Draw "Boat Wind" represented by a 5 knot vector south. Draw 14 knot true wind from the SW acting N.E. to meet the Boat Wind vector. Draw the resultant. It is shorter than true wind and acting on the luff of the sail at an angle farther forward than true wind.

Tide and current

The current in a river or resulting from tide can affect a boat's course in seemingly strange ways. Predicting a boat's actual course becomes simple if you think of the boat velocity and current velocity as two components of a velocity vector triangle. The resultant of their vector addition will be the "course made good".

1) A boat heading North at 5 knots can be represented by a vector 5 units long using a convenient scale to represent knots.

2) The current is moving South West at 3 knots over the ground. Draw a 3 unit vector SW from the point of the boat vector.

3) The resultant joins the two open ends as shown. Its length is measured to find the actual speed and direction the boat travels.

If the velocity vector diagram is plotted on a nautical chart, the actual course can be measured using parallel rulers to transfer he course to a compass rose and read the heading.

Problem

4 knot current is running East caused by the tide and a boat to wishes to sail North East. What course should the skipper steer allow for the drift? The boat speed in the water is 5 knots. Solution: Since the actual course sailed is the resultant vector of a triangle in which the 2 components are boat velocity and current velocity, plot what is known. From the starting point draw 2 components, one starting where the first finishes. Plot a 4 knot tide velocity vector and from its point draw a radius equal to the boat speed vector length until it intersects the resultant course required. This will determine the angle of the boat heading. A line parallel to the boat vector passing through the centre of a compass rose will give the heading.

Force vectors

A Force is a push or pull measured in lbs. or kilograms. A pull of 5 lbs is the same as if a 5 lb weight was hanging from a spring scale and exerting a force of 5 lbs.

A Force Vector is a line drawn to scale to represent a force acting in the direction indicated. That force must be resisted by an equal and opposite force or the object will move. To simplify the discussion, assume no motion takes place.

Consider a chair on carpet so that it does not move easily. "A" pushes or Pulls on the chair toward North.

Add to that a Pull by "B" towards the East. It seems logical that "C" could have used less force than A & B together to pull with an equivalent force towards the N.E.

We can use a force vector to represent each force component on paper, drawn to scale. Choose a scale 1 unit - 1 lb force.

Force Vector diagram using Vector addition.

1) Draw force AB - 5 units long North.
2) Draw force BC - 7 units long East.
3) Join AC and measure the length. This is the Resultant Vector.

AB and BC are components at right angles to each other. AD & DC could have been drawn from "A" to get the same resultant AC. ABCD is a parallelogram of forces,

Problem

If AC had been given and we knew AB & BC were at right angles and AB bears North, Find the value of AB and BC or resolve the resultant into its components.

1) Draw AC 8.5 units long -- the resultant vector.
2) Draw lines North and East through A.
3) Draw lines South and East through C to Form a parallelogram,
4) The length of vector AB and BC is determined by the intersection of adjacent sides. Use the same scale used to draw the resultant to measure the components.

The development of forces on a sail will be shown later. The forces are all combined into one resultant force acting approximately at right angles to the boom or sail chord for the purpose of showing the effect on the boat. Vectors are used to show how the resultant is represented by forward forces that drive the boat and side forces that tend to heel the boat.

Draw a mainsail on a reaching course. Its resultant is drawn X units long at right angles to the sail. Each component must be either parallel or perpendicular to the boat centreline. Draw dotted lines to show direction of component vectors. Draw two parallel lines opposite to them to intersect the arrow point of the resultant forming a parallelogram. This determines the length of the driving force AB and the heeling force AD.

From the above examples it can be seen that the component vectors are equal to the ones parallel and opposite. The parallelogram is a trick to show the equivalent of vector addition to find component vector length. It is better to have the components acting from the same point as the resultant.

Any raft or boat with a sail can be pushed ahead by a following wind. The rate of speed it reaches is determined not only by the wind speed and sail area, but by the friction created by the craft moving through the water. Many factors affect the amount of friction or resistance, but its speed is always less than the wind speed.

Any modern sailboat will sail against the wind at approximately a 45° angle to the true wind or on a reaching course. The wind on the sails causes forces acting to leeward approximately at right angles to the boom. When sailing to windward with the boom-end across the corner of the stern, the sail force will be mostly sideways causing leeway. Due to the angle of the boom there will be some forward force too. Since the boat has a centreboard or keel to resist leeway and is designed for minimum forward resistance, it will naturally move forward.

On a reaching course the boom will be farther out, the sail force angled farther forward and the forward force is greater than the side force. The vector diagram of sailing force shows the relative amount of forward force.

When a boat moves forward in the water, it causes resistance and waves. The harder the sails drive, the faster it tries to go, but rapidly increasing resistance (detailed later) finally limits the maximum speed of any particular design.

A catamaran has two hulls set far apart and designed for minimum resistance. Greater sail force can be developed without capsizing and the limiting speed is often twice that of other types of boats. The reduced resistance allows a catamaran to travel faster than the true wind speed.

Water is heavier, more dense and causes m ore resistance than air as a boat moves through it. An iceboat, with only minimum friction of runners and air resistance can reach 5 times the speed of the true wind. The "Boat Wind" created by this forward motion greatly increases apparent wind. The greater apparent wind increases sail force. This causes a further increase in boat speed and "boat wind" in turn. When resistance of air and runners equals driving force the speed is maintained. An airplane at high altitude with tremendous power and less dense air to resist it, can reach very high speeds.

How and why sail forces develop on a sail will be explained in this chapter. In the past, some theories that seemed logical were used to explain why lift forces developed. They did not conform to the laws of physics.

The results of experiments confirming the venturi effect and Bernoulli's mathematical energy equation will be explained in a simplified form. *Further references for those wishing very technical details will be given,

The invisible driving forces and reacting forces that make a boat go or keep it from accelerating and turning can soon be visualized. It then becomes easier to figure out how to separate the many variables that can improve or hinder good boat speed and boat handling.

How a boat sails

Imagine your boat sitting in the water, not moving, centreboard up, with steady wind blowing at say 10 m.p.h. causing the sails to luff. Turn the boat at an angle of 45° to the wind. The telltales on the shroud will show true wind direction. As you trim the sails until they just stop luffing, air will flow on both sides of the sails and a pressure difference between the two sides is created causing the boat to move slowly in a direction at right angles to the boom without noticeable heeling. If you drop the centreboard, the boat heels, then moves forward.

As forward speed increases, the turbulence around the centreboard becomes smooth flow, and lift to windward is created. Leeway is less. The forward distance becomes so much greater than side slip that leeway is reduced to as little as: 3 degrees. The rudder becomes effective in controlling direction and also helps resist leeway. Crew weight must be adjusted as required to maintain the proper angle of heel.

The forward speed of the boat has however moved the apparent wind forward and the sails begin to luff. The sails are trimmed until luffing stops but the problem is, what is the best heading and trim compromise? By trimming the end of the boom over the corner of the boat as a start and then trimming the jib until it almost backwinds the mainsail, a reasonable compromise is made. From that point on, when going to windward, it is a matter of steering to maintain the jib at the point of almost luffing and observing boat speed. If sails are not adjusted correctly or the boat is being sailed too close to the wind, it will slow down and the heading should be eased a few degrees and sails readjusted to suit.

A lot of sailing experience and preferably another equal boat to tune up with, is excellent for finding your optimum windward settings by trial and error. Sail along beside the other boat about 3 boat lengths apart. The other boat must have settings unchanged while you try jib and main adjustments until speed and pointing angle improve. Note these settings, mark sheets for future use in that condition. Also try to be conscious of the feel of the speed of the boat. Look at the wake for evidence of leeway. These optimum settings should be found with balanced helm. Adjust sails to avoid stalling and luffing of the jib and backwinding of the mainsail. New optimum settings will likely be required for different wind velocities and sea conditions.

Simple Theory of what causes Sail Forces

A sail or airplane wing, because of its curved shape, bends more of the air approaching it around the convex side. When an airplane airfoil or wing is at the correct angle to the air flowing over it, lift force is created. Greater speed causes greater lift force. A deeper curve also increases lift force, up to a point.

A similar force is created towards the outer Curve or lee side of a sail when it is trimmed to cause air to flow smoothly along both sides. There are 6 (six) steps to consider in the change of the apparent wind into a force in a different direction to drive the boat. Many boats can go to windward at only 30 degrees from the apparent wind or, 45 degrees from the true wind direction. The steps are listed below, then a more technical discussion of why it all happens will follow: See drawing.

1) Air tends to deflect around the lee side of the sail and less around the windward side causing a change in air velocity on each side.

2) The increase in velocity on the lee side causes a suction or drop of air pressure close to the sail called the venturi effect.

3) A decrease of air velocity on the windward side has the opposite effect and pressure increases above atmospheric pressure.

4) The opposite pressures on each side result in a total force over the area of the sail acting to leeward and tending to push the boat sideways and slightly ahead.

5) If the centreboard is down to resist the side force, the remaining forward force drives the boat ahead, because forward resistance is much less than the side resistance of the keel.

6) Forward speed increases the resistance forces on the boat until they equal the driving force, resulting in constant speed.

Why forces are created on a sail.

To understand this theory, a brief explanation of the terms involving energy, pressure and force will be helpful.

Why and how sail forces are created by the wind

Forces on a sail are created when the wind causes a pressure difference between the windward and leeward sides of the sail. The force always acts at right angles to the sail surface no matter what angle the wind approaches the sail. On a run, the wind strikes the sail nearly at right angles and builds up a pressure that pushes the sail. When it hits the sail, the wind slows down and some of its velocity energy changes to pressure energy to create a force.

Force and pressure are related by a very simple formula. When the wind pushes on a sail running ahead of the wind, the pressure may be only 1 lb. per square foot of sail area. A sail of 100 square foot area would then have a total force created of 100 lbs.

On a beat or reach, sail pressure and forces are developed in surface instead of against it. The size of the force developed on the wind velocity and size, shape and trim of the sail. In the same wind, much greater force can be developed on a beat than on a run. It is important to know how the sail forces on both sides are created. Sail shape adjustment and trim can then be more logically made for maximum sail force.

There are two sources of energy in the wind, *pressure* and *velocity energy.* Wind energy is used to increase the air pressure on the windward side and to lower pressure on the leeward side of the sail.

Pressure Energy is the potential energy contained in the pressure of the atmosphere. Atmospheric pressure is caused by the force of gravity compressing the air against the earth. It is there whether there is wind or not. Compared to a perfect vacuum its pressure is about 14.7 lbs per square inch (nearly a ton per square foot).

Potential energy is the ability to do work. Atmospheric pressure can do work when it causes a force that is able to move something such as a sail and boat. A sail has atmospheric pressure on both sides. When the pressure on one side is changed, the higher pressure on one side causes a sail force. A very slight difference of pressure over much of the sail area will create a significant force to move the sail and boat.

Potential energy technically is mass x acceleration of gravity x distance the mass moves.

The other source of wind energy is the energy of motion or velocity energy. Air has weight and a unit volume of moving air contains both potential and velocity energy. Energy cannot be created or lost. When flowing smoothly, it can be converted from velocity energy to potential pressure energy without appreciable loss, as it flows around a sail.

An example of exchange of energy can be seen clearly when a weight is used as a pendulum. At both ends of the swing its velocity is zero. As it approaches the centre of the swing, its velocity is maximum and its potential energy due to gravity is zero. In between zero and maximum velocity it has both potential and velocity energy the same as a moving airstream. As the velocity of the air at any point increases, the potential or pressure energy decreases without loss of total energy.

In the drawing, the flow lines indicate that the air from A deflects around the leeward side. This pattern is started when the trim of the sail causes a slightly higher pressure on the windward side. Air approaching the mast deflects around the leeside. This further increases the difference in pressure on the two sides and deflects even more air to the lee side.

The equal quantities of air in the stream meeting the sail at A & C meet unequal areas at B & D. Air at B must squeeze through a narrower space. Density of air at these velocities remains constant so velocity must increase. Air from C expanding to the larger area at D, must slow down to fill the space.

Bernoulli, a scientist in 1738, established that the sum of static and velocity or dynamic pressures at the same point is constant within an air stream. If air flow or water flow is not turbulent, energy is not lost as it moves through a changing area pattern. Bernoulli's mathematical energy equation proves that a change in velocity at a point must result in opposite change in pressure at the same point.

Bernoulli's Energy equation assumes that no significant energy is lost in the change of velocity from A to B and from C to D. Therefore the energy (E) due to the pressure (P) at A plus the energy due to velocity at A equals the energy due to pressure at B plus the energy due to velocity at B.

If EV_b increases, EPb must decrease to equal the same total energy at A. Similarly $EP_c + EV_c = EP_d + EV_d$ for the windward side. If EV_d decreases, EP_d must increase to equal the same total energy at C. The pressure change is greatest on the lee for two reasons.

1) The velocity change close to the sail on the lee side is greater than the velocity change close to the sail on the windward side.

2) Since pressure converts to velocity, and vice versa, in proportion to the velocity change squared, the pressure change on the lee side becomes nearly (4) four times as great as on the windward side.

As soon as a sail is allowed to stall or flow becomes separated on the lee side, that advantage is lost.

Demonstration of the lee side pressure drop

To demonstrate the reduced pressure on the lee side of the sail, we can use a glass of water and a small piece of transparent plastic straw or glass tube. Put one end of the straw into the water vertically and note that the level of the water is the same inside and outside of the straw. Both surfaces are subject to atmospheric and barometric pressure. Blow a high velocity stream of air, at right angles to the straw, across its open top. Have someone observe the water level in the straw to see how much it rises. Blow harder and it will rise higher. The velocity across the straw reduced the static pressure acting on the water inside, while the atmospheric pressure on the surface of the water in the glass pushed the water up the straw. This is the same effect that occurs when velocity is increased on the lee side of a sail and pressure is reduced.

How sail forces act on a boat

The forces acting on each side of a sail are shown above. They it vary in strength according to how much change of velocity, occurs at that point. The longer arrows on the lee side show up to four times greater force and the proper effect of a jib slot on the mainsail increases the lee side force even more. The resultant force representing all the forces acting to leeward is shown near the centre of area or centre of effort. Its direction is slightly ahead of a right angle to the chord of the sail.

The forces on the mainsail pull on the mast and mainsheet. The jib forces are transferred to the boat at tack and clew and pull on the mast at the hounds or attachment of the jib halyard. The sail forces of one or more sails are resolved into one resultant force at the combined centre of effort for convenience of comparison with the centre of lateral resistance. The angle of the resultant force compared to the centreline of the boat, depends on the boat's point of sail. On a reach, for example, the angle points farther forward than on a close hauled course. Side force becomes less, and forward force more.

Sail forces driving and tending to heel the boat must be resisted by a resultant of side and aft resistance forces. They must act directly opposite or the boat will turn. When the centre of effort is slightly aft of the resisting forces or centre of lateral resistance, the boat has weather helm. Weather helm simply means that sufficient rudder side-force is imposed to make CE & CLR line up by pulling the tiller to windward until the boat holds a straight course. When tacking or turning, the rudder causes a side force at the stern and the boat pivots around the centreboard.

The side component of resistance is the sum of centreboard, rudder and hull resistance. Balance affecting turning can be changed by moving the centreboard fore or aft, by turning the rudder or by moving weight in the boat to change the fore and aft trim. Weight moved forward increases resistance to leeway forward and raises the stern decreasing its resistance to leeway. Lee and weather helm are thus affected by changing resistance fore and aft as well as changing the position of sail effort fore and aft.

It can be seen that the angle of the boom, determined by whether the boat is close hauled or broad reaching, changes the angle at which the two resultants act compared to the boat's centreline. As the boom swings out, the intersection of the resultant with the centreline moves aft, making it very difficult with a single sail to avoid using rudder to balance the forces. If the boat is heeled to windward the CE moves in and avoids rudder angle which increases drag.

Resistance to forward speed

If there were no water resistance on the hull, the sail driving force would cause the boat to keep increasing speed. Actually, forward resistance increases very rapidly as speed increases until the resistance force equals sail driving force and the boat maintains speed. The factors affecting speed vary in relative amount at different speeds and with different hulls. These factors are: wave making resistance, skin friction, hull heeling friction, leeway resistance and wind friction.

In light air total resistance is low, because speed is low. Apparent wind increases over true wind speed in light air because boat speed is a higher ratio to wind speed than in heavy air. In heavy air, boat speed is maximum but wind speed, may increase to many times, and boat speed cannot increase. A hull may have a maximum hull-speed of 5 mph with a wind of from 12 to 30 mph; but may have a speed of 3 mph with only a 6 mph wind.

The biggest factor affecting this is wave Making resistance The bow wave builds up and prevents further speed increase unless planing can be induced in a dinghy. The maximum hull speed is based on waterline length. Speed in knots equals speed-length ratio of about 1.34 times the square root of the waterline length in feet. A 16 foot boat has a maximum hull speed of 1.34?16= 5.36 knots.

Skin friction of hull, centreboard and rudder increases as the(square of the velocity. In light air it is small, but relative to wave making resistance it is very significant. In heavy air and when planing especially, the skin friction becomes very significant in limiting hull speed. The *heeling* of a hull especially a dinghy which is designed to be sailed almost flat *causes resistance.* As the boat heels, the underwater shape changes and must push more water out of the way on one side. This not only slows the boat but causes turning effects requiring rudder correction and increased drag. In very light air at slow speed the „resistance is not significant.

Leeway resistance may be very small or at times quite significant. After a tack, when heeled too much, or when pinching too close to the wind, the boat tends to push through the water at an angle. The streamline shape is poorer at an angle and the flow of water is less smooth and causes resistance. This is one reason footing is faster than pinching.

Wind resistance is the friction of the wind on the hull, shrouds, mast, sail, and crew. If the sail luffs it also increases the wind resistance. In light air it is a small factor, but in heavy wind it is much more significant.

A dinghy with light enough weight and flat aft section skims on the water in strong winds when reaching, and lifts on to its bow wave. It is planing when all the buoyant lift becomes dynamic lift (supported by skimming). The theoretical hull speed can more than double, and bow wave resistance is no longer the largest speed limiting factor.

The importance of limiting friction-causing-forces cannot be underestimated. In light air and planing conditions, large improvements in hull speed can be achieved with the same sail forces. In some cases the extra speed increases apparent wind speed and driving force.

A keelboat is normally limited to a maximum hull

speed based on the waterline length formula. Surfing in waves can increase that slightly. The hull is designed to sail at an angle of heel that does not cause unnecessary hull friction. If heeling beyond that, sail area must be reduced to maintain hull speed. There is turning balance in which sails due to their position and forces must be resisted equally by underwater forces. There is also weight balance which is counteracting sail heeling forces with a heavy keel or crew weight on the windward side. Since the sail force is much higher than the centre of lateral resistance of the hull, a couple or turning moment is created. This must be balanced, preferably while upright, with a crew weight acting as far from the centre of buoyancy as possible. Weight balance is when sail force couple and weight force couple are equal. If not equal, the boat is capsizing or righting.

Balance—Lee helm and weather helm

The term "Balance" can mean the effect of crew or keel weight when used to counteract the heeling caused by the wind on the sails. Here, however, we refer to the balance of turning forces caused by sails which are resisted in the right location by centreboard and underwater surfaces to prevent turning. For example, if a sail plan is too far forward, the wind will tenc to push the bow to leeward unless the rudder is turned so that the tiller or helm is too leeward to keep it steering straight. This is called lee helm. Lee helm must be avoided when going to windward because the force of water on the rudder when turned to windward, tends to push the boat to leeward. Weather helm of 4°-8° helps to push a boat slightly to windward to reduce leeway.

Centre of effort

The CE of each sail can be found on paper by finding its centre of area. Draw the sail plan and boat to scale. Draw a line from each corner of the sail to the midpoint of the opposite side. The intersection of these lines is the CE of the sail and close to „the point where the resultant of all the forces acts. The CE of the sail plan of a sloop is on the line joining the CE of each sail nearer the larger sail and in the ratio of their areas; e.g. if the One is 3 units long and the ratio of mainsail area to jib area is 2 to 1, divide the line in 3 parts and locate the CE of the sail plan from the CE of the jib.

Centre of lateral resistance

The CLR is the point on the hull centreline at which the combined lateral resistance of the hull, centreboard and rudder acts.

Try a simple experiment at the dock to find the CLR in smooth water without wind or sails but with centreboard down and rudder in the centre. Push or pull the side of the hull at the Point where you find the centreline moves abeam evenly without turning. That is the CLR. By moving weight forward in the boat to change the waterline or the centreboard aft, you can see the new position of the CLR. The objective of CE and CLR study is to get a feel for the factors that tend to affect weather or lee helm by moving these two centres in relation to each other. Also try pushing the boat straight ahead in smooth water without a rudder and experiment with the turning effect of the boat heeled to one side or the other. You will find you can steer by the angle of heel in most boats.

How to increase weather helm—move CE aft or CLR forward.

(1) Trim mainsail and ease jib.

(2) Rake mast aft by moving mast step forward and easing forestay.

(3) Move draft aft by releasing any cunningham or easing main halyard.

(4) Use a smaller jib or increase the size or power of the mainsail.

(5) Tighten mainsail leech with boomvang.

(6) Move crew weight forward.

(7) Move centreboard forward.

(8) Increase leeward heel angle in light air and drifters.

How to decrease weather helm -- move CE forward or CLR aft.

(1) Trim jib and ease mainsail.

(2) Decrease rake.

(3) Move draft in sails forward or increase draft of jib.

(4) Use Genoa instead of working jib or reduce size or power of mainsail.

(5) Ease leech tension and increase twist.

(6) Move crew weight aft.

(7) Move or pivot centreboard aft.

(8) Reduce heeling to leeward or even heel to windward.

All these factors change the relative positions of CE and CLR. The angle of heel can quickly separate these two centres causing weather helm. The CE of the sails moves to leeward as viewed at right angles to the boom. At the same time the centreboard tilts to windward and the underwater shape dips lower near the bow moving CLR forward. See drawing. On a reach this effect is more pronounced. When heeled to windward these two centres move toward each other and maintain balanced helm.

3

BOAT HANDLING

Review of tacking

Basic objective

The basic objective when tacking is to retain as much boat speed as possible and have maximum progress to windward. This is determined by the relative significance of momentum and resistance factors. They vary according to conditions and determine the best tacking technique. Boat speed should always be the maximum possible before the tack and regained quickly if lost after the tack to avoid leeway.

Momentum

Momentum carries a boat farther to windward in light air and smooth water than in heavy air and waves. This is because resistance is less at lower speed despite the fact that momentum is also less. Therefore, tacking in very light air must be slower after speed is built up to its maximum by good trimming and by footing more. In waves, keep it flat and foot faster before tacking to increase momentum and reduce leeway. In waves, the maximum speed is after you bear off down the back of a wave. The best time to tack, however, is on the crest of the wave, so that momentum is not decreasing as the sails stop driving in the tack. Try to be around before the next wave hits the boat.

Resistance

This is the factor that slows the boat. In light wind, the main factor could be the turbulence of the rudder and hull when turned too fast. Wind resistance and wave and hull resistance are very small. In medium winds, however, these add significant resistance to overcome increased speed and momentum. The best turning speed is judged by minimum loss of speed in practice. In heavy wind, before the tack, boat speed is maximum and total resistance is also a maximum. During the tack, the sails luff, drive stops, and high wind resistance slows the boat even more quickly. So tack quickly to keep the slowing time as short as possible.

Rudder resistance

The rudder should be moved slowly when turning in lighter air to let the boat follow its direction and reduce turbulence to a minimum. In heavier air it must be turned faster and farther, but try to start and finish the turn more slowly to retain smooth flow and avoid a stalled rudder and drag. In larger waves, however, rudder resistance is less significant than other losses, so be deliberate and tack precisely in the best spot. Rudder shape should be airfoil cross-section to reduce turbulence and give a more sensitive feeling when turning. The tiller should fit snuggly in the rudder head to avoid play and to be able to feel the helm.

Relearning how to tack

Everyone has developed some means of "getting about" and changing hands by cleating the sheet, letting go of the tiller or whatever. It will pay to examine and practise this simple method that can be used in any condition for sure positive control. Take a tiller and two normal chairs facing each other, side deck width apart. Have a 3/8° sheet available as led from the centreboard trunk just ahead of the helmsman position. Pivot the tiller in a chair on the boat centreline.

(a) Using the tiller, no hiking tiller, and no mainsheet. Hold the tiller in the aft hand while sitting on one chair.

   (1) Push the tiller to leeward and move the aft foot across the boat centreline facing forward.

   (2) Turn the body more than 90° and move the body across the centreline, pivoting on the aft foot and crouching, head down, but looking forward.

   (3) Move the tiller back to the boat centreline as the sail fills on the other side. Have the other hand waiting behind the back.

   (4) Transfer the tiller to that hand and sit down.

(b) Repeat using a mainsheet in the forward hand, tiller in aft hand.

   (1) Push the tiller to leeward and move the aft foot across as before.

   (2) Turn the body more than 90° pivoting on the aft foot.

   (3) Move the tiller behind the back to the centre as the tack is finished and transfer it to the hand holding the sheet. Watch the heading and jib luff.

   (4) Move the hand around to your front and take the mainsheet, now in the forward hand.

   (5) Complete turning the body and sit down. Tuck toes under hiking straps if hiking.

(c) Repeat using a tiller extension with swivel fitting and no mainsheet.

(1) Hold the tiller extension approximately 18" from the end of the tiller.

(2) Push the tiller away to leeward with the extension as you move the aft foot across facing forward. Swivel extension 180°.

(3) Move the tiller back to the centreline behind the back.

(4) Grab the tiller extension with the new aft hand and sit down.

(d) Repeat again, this time using a mainsheet and tiller extension. Assume the mainsheet is led to the midboom position and down to the centreboard trunk.

(1) Hold the hiking tiller in the aft hand and the sheet in the forward hand.

(2) Push the tiller to leeward as the aft foot moves across facing forward.

(3) Move the tiller extension around 1800, then the tiller to the centreline as the tack is finished.

(4) Grab the extension with the sheet hand on the side nearest the tiller end.

(5) Release the hand that was holding the extension behind the back and grab the sheet in front of you. The key is to exchange hands at the last moment.

(6) Move back on the windward side and sit down.

Repeat this faster and faster and now you are ready for anything. Don't forget to duck when the boom comes across and look forward rather than down at the bottom of the boat. Note: The space between end of tiller and centreboard trunk in different boats varies.

Roll tacking is a method of getting the sails to drive on one tack until the boat is almost on the new tack and letting them snap to the new position. To do this you have to roll the boat to windward as the boat is tacking. The apparent wind will be on the same side of the sails at an angle to keep them full and driving. When the roll is suddenly stopped, the apparent wind suddenly comes from the new windward side and the wind establishes flow on the new tack immediately. This technique is so effective in some boats in light air that progress to windward is slightly improved, rather than slowed, compared to conventional tacking. The centreboard levers the boat slightly to windward. Precise timing by both helmsman and crew is achieved by practise. Roll tacking is commonly used in dinghy racing.

Roll tacking procedure

(1) Heel the boat 15° to leeward.

(2) Ease the tiller slightly to leeward to allow the boat to start to head up.

(3) Before the jib luffs, on prepractised signal, helmsman and crew start to roll the boat to windward smoothly, keeping sails full.

(4) As the boat passes the eye of the wind, the tiller should just start to return to the centreline to prevent it going too far.

(5) Before the boat heels 25° to windward start to move back.

(6) Crew, with a jib sheet in each hand, releases driving sheet only when it collapses and trims other sheet immediately.

(7) Helmsman stops turn at the new course and moves to windward to get a slight drive from the return roll to flat or upright. This rolling must be done smoothly to avoid causing centreboard turbulence.

In slightly choppy water, easing the sails for a moment at the end of the turn and trimming as speed picks up is better. In a drifter you may want to remain heeled a little on the new tack. The technique takes practise. Timing changes with increase in wind velocity. In stronger wind there may only be time enough to hike to windward to give a partial roll, otherwise a capsize could occur on the new tack.

Roll tacking is fun and tends to improve all tacking. New awareness of keeping sails driving longer, avoiding heeling to leeward before tacking, and precise teamwork is achieved.

Crewing while tacking

Crewing with any new skipper requires some practise to get used to signals and timing and variations of technique. A good crew will always try to do the following:

(1) Keep the boat flat before a standard tack.

(2) Be ready to tack within a few seconds, releasing jib sheet from jam cleat first.

(3) Be conscious of which foot to put across the centreboard trunk first to face the right way.

(4) To be aware of jib settings on one tack and automatically make the same ones on the other side after a tack.

(5) Avoid backing the jib, sitting or stepping on jib sheets.

(6) Keep watch for other boats that a sudden tack could suddenly put in the way.

(7) If the boat should get in irons, be able to back the jib on the correct side to push the bow away.

Gybing

Gybing, to get from one tack to the other, with wind astern, Must be fully controlled. In light air it is simple, but in heavy air improper technique can easily cause capsize. There are four kinds of gybes; the accidental gybe, the light air straight line gybe, the roll-to-steer gybe for minimum rudder drag, an the heavy air controlled gybe to avoid capsize or broaching.

The basic causes of gybing capsize

Sail forces while gybing, must be pushing as much as possible in the direction the boat is moving. Side forces in heavy air can cause a capsize especially when the crew are near the centre of the boat. Sail forces act at right angles to the chord of the sail regardless of the wind direction.

(1) The force that often gets out of control is centrifugal force. It is the force on the mast and boat directed to the outside of a turn when the boat is moving and is resisted by the centreboard. A motor boat simply banks to the inside and skids on its chine, while a dinghy literally trips over its centreboard and leans out on a turn. The sailboat heels on the same side as the tiller moves to, for example moving the tiller to leeward, the boat heels to leeward. Bearing away by pulling the tiller to windward will make it try to heel to windward. The greater the speed the greater the heeling force.

(2) As the boom swings over during a gybe, it suddenly causes a heeling force when stopped by the sheet or

shroud. It reduces the force when the crew can slow down the boom movement as it crosses a small boat.

(3) A heeled boat lifts most of the rudder out of the water. The angle of entry of the rudder, when heeled and turned, stalls or causes turbulence and has little effect on turning the boat. The natural hard-over turning then only increases the braking effect or drag of the rudder and increases heeling pressure on the sails.

(4) When racing around a gybing mark, the tendency is to gybe and round as soon as possible. This is where many capsizes occur. Even when a capsize is averted by a controlled gybe, exchanging hands on tiller and sheet must be quick so you can hike and trim for immediate planing. It may be advantageous to change hands before a gybe and practise it beforehand to make it easy.

(5) If the wind shifts on a run and causes the boat to sail by-the-fee, it might gybe accidentally. If you suddenly head up to prevent this, it may start the boom moving across. It may not be possible to ease the mainsheet if the boom is against the shroud. If it is a single hander without shrouds, easing the mainsail a little too much could cause part of the sail to drive to windward and capsize. The best solution is to do a controlled gybe immediately if there is sea room. In a sloop the crew can usually hold the boom just enough to allow the boat to be headed up until the wind is dead aft.

(6) On boats with rear traveller, mainsheets often catch on the corner of the transom. This restricts the boom from running out to the shroud. It is a nuisance and could cause side sail forces. In a Laser for example, when gybing in any weather, you must always give

a sharp tug on the sheet as the boom is coming over to prevent this.

(7) Mast rolling from side to side on a run, just prior to a gybe, must be stopped. It is caused by alternate forces acting to windward, then to leeward. Trying to shift crew weight and over-correcting can make it worse. Pull the mainsail in a little, move aft more and drop the centreboard to halfway down.

(8) A problem experienced more in single handers than sloops is capsizing to windward on a run. The shroud does not limit the boom position. A slack boom vang allows more twist at the top of the mainsail. Either way, if the sail force is to windward the boat will heel to windward. Heeling to windward causes the hull to turn and sail by-the-lee, rudder is ineffective and a sudden gybe can occur. if you do not duck, in time a crash helmet would not protect you from the boom. 1st rule in heavy weather is tie a stopper knot in the mainsheet to limit boom angle. 2nd. Avoid sailing straight down wind and waves by gybing and broad reaching down wind. It's safer and more fun surfing on the waves. Rule 3. Tighten boom vang to reduce twist of the mainsail.

(9) When gybing in large waves, pick the right time. If you gybe on top of a wave, wind pressure is maximum, boat speed is minimum and steering control is less positive. Always try to gybe when the boat has just run down a wave to increase speed and reduce pressure on the sails.

Beating

Basic objective—To sail for optimum progress to windward. The following skills must be practised on the water.

(1) Sense wind direction and velocity changes.

(2) Steer for optimum balance between pointing and speed.

(3) Make adjustments for sensitive weather helm and speed.

(4) Maintain constant angle of heel for the condition.

Many of these facts are interrelated. To be able to sail an optimum windward course, a lot of practice and concentration is required. As time goes by, many of the skills developed become almost automatic reactions making it easier and more enjoyable. Improved windward technique is a great asset especially for the racing sailor. Meeting nature's challenge of wind and water is very rewarding.

Wind changes

To sail to windward well, the sails must be set at a certain angle to the boat and must meet the apparent wind at the right angle to suit them. The apparent wind angle as seen on a vector diagram is determined by the direction of the boat to the wind and the speeds of both. A change in either wind direction or speed will change the apparent wind angle. When we sail to windward the helmsman must constantly change the heading of the boat to suit the apparent wind changes.

The most significant difference between beating and reaching technique is that when beating, you must sense the precise optimum beating angle to the apparent wind continually. You must steer along the changing line with jib trim fixed at the optimum setting, usually cleated. The optimum trim angle only changes when the conditions change. For example, in smooth water, medium air, trim as close as is practical without losing boat speed. In waves and heavy air, the angle should be increased slightly for footing to make the best net progress to windward by minimizing leeway.

When the jib is trimmed for beating, it is very easy to slowly head up and see it begin to luff then you bear away a degree or two. The problem some sailors have at first is that when stalling, even 10° off course, the luff looks the same. You must test slowly for that slight indication of luffing every few seconds or, use wool indicators that are even more sensitive and move when air flow is not perfect on both sides. It is vital to sense the line of the optimum windward course by steering to the luff of the jib. In very light air it pays to divide wool or nylon yarn into lighter more sensitive separate strands a little shorter to sense where the optimum course is.

Steering—In order to have sensitive response to the tiller movements, there must be no play between hiking tiller, tiller, rudder head, blade or pintles and gudgeon.

The need for tiller movements must be sensed soon enough to make slight corrections. Over-correction in steering, results in loss of power and less progress to windward most of the time. Under-correction of steering in big waves results in noticeable loss of boat speed by not playing the waves correctly. Take charge of the tiller, steer quickly, and ignore rudder turbulence at that moment. The wave will slow your boat more than the rudder turbulence. The same applies when a header requires quick rudder action to prevent luffing and loss of power. There are three ways, besides jib luff trim to sense sensitive steering at the best angle between pointing and speed. One is by the feel of the helm, another by a tendency to heel more, a third is increased sheet tension. Sensitivity to these methods requires practice. The optimum angle to the wind causes more driving and heeling force. If the jib is losing force, the boat heels less, signalling the helmsman to bear away slightly. To confirm it, there will be slightly less pressure on the helm. You can begin to feel the decrease and increase in pull as you slowly and continually move the helm back and forth slightly with a very light touch. This will allow you to feel if there is more weather helm, or less, as you move the tiller slightly to windward. It does not allow time for over correction. It's like focussing a pair of binoculars too far and too close to find the optimum focus.

Adjustments for sensitive helm and speed

Weather helm is the slight pull you feel on the tiller of a well-balanced boat when held about 40 to windward. This helps a boat go to windward because there is a slight pressure on the fee side of the rudder and lift on the windward side if it is shaped correctly. When the tiller is held on centreline the boat should head up. Only push to leeward for a sudden lift that would otherwise cause sails to stall and lose power.

In light air, 3-4 knots, a boat has less weather helm. The centre of effort is farther forward when flow becomes detached farther aft. This is corrected by heeling to leeward, moving crew weight forward and slightly increasing the jib trim. Heeling does not cause more friction at such low speeds.

In heavy winds, too much weather helm is caused mainly by heeling too much and partly by a tight leech on the mainsail. Sail it flat and let the leech twist. Pivoting the centreboard up a little helps reduce heeling and weather helm. Let the jib luff a little in the gusts. It tends to reduce weather helms a little and gains distance to windward as the boat heads up slightly. A boat can be sailed at a constant angle of heel by sensing the pull on the helm. The tendency to heel more before the jib luffs will signal course correction required.

Speed of the boat in the water must be constantly sensed. It takes time. It is just a feeling you should be aware of. The wake will probably show signs of more leeway when you pinch too much and slow up. Pointing angle does not mean good progress to windward if the boat does not have good speed. It will travel at a slight angle through the water and the actual course will be lower. This is particularly true in waves or chop. Ease sheets slightly and foot more.

Good pointing requires a tight straight luff, jib draft in the middle and not too full. Trim in at the foot and let the leech twist to stop backwinding of the mainsail. Not all boat classes will have the same optimum pointing angle; some do not allow inboard jib sheeting. Light air requires flatter sails up to about 3 knots, then increased apparent wind speed to windward allows fuller shape that will maintain attached flow. Use telltales in several locations, including the leech, to tell when flow is attached or not. When the sail is too full in a drifter or heavy air, the flow will break away half way back on the mainsail and reduce sail power.

Flat sails work best in smooth water (0-3 knots) and when overpowered at higher speeds. It fits in with pointing ability too, chop and waves require footing and more power with fuller draft.

Weight balance—The crew should sit forward to the shrouds in moderate and heavy air and smooth water. The bow should be down an inch or two below its design water line. In waves that must be ridden over, the crew and skipper should sit aft a little but slide forward on the crest of a wave and aft going up and down a wave. Angle of heel should be constant to suit conditions. Sail it flat except in a drifter. Some classes claim the optimum angle of heel is 10 or 15 degrees, but beyond that, compounded losses affect progress to windward severely. Keel boats are designed for heeling a little, and lengthen water line and increase hull speed a little compared to sailing upright.

The sequence of losses in a dinghy goes as follows, when a gust hits while beating: If allowed to heel too much the rudder lifts half out of the water and depending on its shape will tend to drag. The lee bow-wave friction created slows the boat and causes weather helm. The tiller is pulled harder and the rudder acts as a brake. The centreboard has less effective depth and stalls as leeway increases. The sails have less forward driving force. The mainsail cannot be eased more because the boom hits the water. Mast weight when heeled increases and hiking is less effective. The only action to prevent a capsize is to release the jib sheet. The boat will have almost stopped when it rights. Sheet in, hike and get moving quickly.

The following points summarize technique to sail it flat when heavy.

(1) Tighten outhaul to flatten mainsail and move jib fairlead outboard and aft to open slot and flatten the jib.

(2) Ease main traveller, and in a gust, ease mainsheet to reduce heeling.

(3) Adjust boom vang to allow mainsail twist, ease jib sheet to allow jib twist and reduce backwinding of the mainsail.

(4) Anticipate a heeling gust on the water and both crew should hike hard together so the boat is flat when the gust hits.

(5) Feel changes of weather helm and head up before the jib stalls, even letting part of the jib luff.

(6) Maintain boat speed by bearing off before it slows too much. Ease mainsail, if necessary, to prevent heeling.

(7) Practise technique until the boat is flat in any wind velocity.

(8) Steer positively in gusts and waves to prevent stalling or over-correcting and to keep up boat speed.

Beating in waves

The critical points are maintaining boat speed and steering over the waves. The major problem is the energy absorbed in lifting the weight up to 2 to 5 ft. A single hander weighing 300 lbs with skipper or a dinghy up to 1,000 lbs takes a lot of momentum and sail power. The proper method is to steer almost straight up the wave until the bow passes the crest of the wave and start to bear away down the other side to pick up speed. The sail may luff a little, but apparent wind changes as the boat slows and again as it speeds up to partly compensate. A heavy boat does not accelerate as fast, so you will have to bear off less, unless it is possible to ease sheets out each time it bears away to help drive the boat. Tiller action must be very positive especially in short waves. This technique reduces the distance sailed while travelling up the wave and reduces the area of broadside hull being pushed to leeward by the wave as the crest hits the boat. The finer lines of the bow cut into the wave more directly.

Reaching

Reaching is any course between beating and running. Close reaching is different from footing when beating, in that you concentrate on boat speed and do not try to make maximum progress to windward. Reaching reverses the beating technique when wind gets too heavy to keep it flat. Instead of feathering or heading up in gusts, you must ease sheets and bear off, which generates perhaps twice the speed of beating while planing.

The objective in reaching is steering the fastest average course to a destination, not necessarily in a straight line. For maximum boat speed we must review our techniques for steering, tuning, and trimming, and both weight and helm balance to get maximum driving force and minimum resistance. Keep in mind that driving force is maximum on a close reach, but so is heeling force. In light to medium air, the fastest course is a close reach where apparent wind speed increases and the boat can be kept flat. In heavier and gusty winds, the fastest course is the highest reach you can keep the boat flat on while always sailing in the most wind. This means bearing off in gusts and always heading up above your average direction between gusts. Review the main objectives for boat speed under the following headings:

Steering

(1) In planing conditions, steer to maintain planing as much of the time as possible. Bear off in gusts, up in lulls.

(2) In non-planing conditions, tend to steer a straighter course unless there are periodic or geographic wind shifts. Try to keep the flow on both sides of the main, assisted by the jib for as long as possible. Sailing with stalled sails on a broad reach is the slowest reaching course.

(3) In any weather, always steer to sail in the most wind available. Bearing off 15° from the rhumb line (direct

course) causes very little extra distance. In light air, steer above the rhumb line to get into a breeze, then bear off and sail in it. The boat tends to reach across the lulls the shortest distance in order to stay in the puffs longer.

(4) When a puff or gust hits be sure to keep the boat flat. Anticipate the heeling. Move aft, hike hard, ease the sheets slightly and bear off almost simultaneously. If the boat heels, the bow wave prevents planing and the gust may be gone before you recover. Progress may be only half of that with proper technique. Steer towards the direction the mast is heeling.

(5) Steering sensitivity to avoid rudder drag is essential for minimum resistance. Maintain neutral helm, avoid sudden movements and heeling. Weather helm can be caused by heeling to leeward or too much centreboard down. Try sailing with rudder fixed amidships and steer by the angle of heel. it will make you more conscious of avoiding oversteering resistance. A slight wandering of course is not going to slow the boat, providing you adjust trim to suit.

(6) Steering in waves should take advantage of the momentum gained by running down the front of a wave and planing at an angle across the trough to partly coast up the back of the next. At the top of the wave, sheets eased a little and steering downwind, accelerate down the wave by a quick pump of the mainsail and leaning or sliding forward for a moment. The wave will get under the hull and push it forward. Head up, sheet in, and plane at an angle down into the trough and bear off up the back of the next, weight leaning aft until it reaches the top. If the wind is marginal and the waves high and travelling fast, stay on the face of the wave and surf on one

wave as long as you can. The apparent wind keeps changing rapidly as boat speed and angle change, requiring rapid trimming and easing to maintain maximum power. Weight balance is also very important; keep it flat.

Tuning and trimming

(1) Ease the outhaul on a reach about 3 inches except in a drifter or a close reach in heavy air. Maximum driving force is obtained with a 7:1 ratio of chord length to chord depth, fullness or camber. On a close reach when it is heavy, flatten mainsail, ease the vang and the jib sheet to allow more twist to keep it upright. Keep the centreboard ½ way up and play the traveller in gusts, trying to plane as much as possible.

(2) Rarely cleat sails on a reach. They should be constantly adjusted to prevent stalling or luffing. The apparent wind angle will be changing very often whenever you change course, when the boat changes speed, or when the wind changes speed or direction. Watch the luff and telltales on the sails.

(3) To initiate planing in marginal conditions, you must be ready to balance heeling by trimming or easing sails. As the boat bears away to lift on to a plane, you may have to ease the main a moment then pull in sharply, or pump it to give extra thrust as it speeds up. Once on the plane, you can head up and trim more and still keep the boat upright.

(4) The crew must be ready to trim the jib as required for all the changes of apparent wind without command. The helmsman has enough to do to steer and watch the mainsail. The jib leech often falls off on a reach unless the fairleads are moved forward or a barber haul fairlead is used.

(5) Limit mainsheet length in heavy wind and reduce twist so that heeling forces do not act to windward and cause capsize.

Weight balance

(1) In light air sit forward. Below planing speed, carry weight the same as for beating, and for planing, both crew move two or more feet aft to lift the bow out of the water on to the bow wave.

(2) Keep the boat from heeling enough to cause weather helm.

(3) Heeling in light air does not slow the boat at slow speeds because friction on the hull is small. Heeling can be used to create neutral helm if there is lee helm. In a drifter, heel the boat to leeward to let the sails take their proper shape by gravity.

(4) If a one-man-boat or any boat cannot be sailed on a broad reach with neutral helm, when centreboard is adjusted properly, heel to windward.

(5) Judge fore and aft weight position to eliminate the turbulent effect at the transom, seen when weight is too far aft. This occurs between planing gusts if weight has not moved forward.

Helm balance

(1) Helm balance should be neutral on a reach to reduce any friction caused by the rudder.

(2) Position of centreboard affects helm balance. The rule of thumb should be only enough board down to prevent leeway. Too much on a planing reach causes weather helm. It needs less at higher speeds. Generally 1/3 down on a broad reach and ½ way down on a beam reach in light to moderate air.

(3) A pivoting board has a greater effect on helm balance than a daggerboard. As it moves up, it moves aft tending to compensate for the centre of effort which crosses the centreline farther aft.

(4) A jib winged out to the opposite side from the boom helps to reduce weather helm.

In any boat, it is helpful to learn about balance factors by tying the tiller amidships and balancing with sails, centreboard and weight position.

Running

Running downwind is the slowest point of sail and tends to be more relaxing if the boom is out to the shroud, the whisker pole is set and the wind steady and light. If you are interested in maximum boat speed, however, there arc many points to consider for marginal improvement on a run.

Steering—To minimize turning forces causing rudder drag, you may have to heel the boat to windward for neutral helm. Move crew weight forward, in light air, as far as possible to get the bow down. The helmsman can sit forward as far as the tiller extension allows to reduce wetted surface aft. As boat speed picks up, the bow wave resistance increases, so weight should be moved to the normal position as long as stern drag is avoided.

In planing weather and in waves, there is a tendency to bury the bow from forward sail pressure. Rocking can result, so have one person on each side moved aft, with board at least ½ way down and mainsheet trimmed off the shroud a little. Steering can become critical at high speed. Sudden movements tilt the mast in the same direction by centrifugal force, so you must steer under the sails with sensitivity. Heeling too much causes lee bow wave forces to turn the boat and a broach is possible in heavy wind.

Steering the fastest course is not necessarily a straight line downwind, in some classes. Running is the slowest point of sail, so try to find a way to reach at an angle of at least 15° and gybe back on the other tack. Play the windshifts to avoid sailing by the lee and to get a better angle. A 15° angle causes only a 4% increase in distance. Speed needs only to increase 5% by a faster angle. The advantage is greatest when planing improves the apparent wind angle. Sailing with the puffs and reaching across in the lulls will more than make it up. It does not usually pay to deviate from the straight course in steady medium winds when the boat is at maximum hull speed. It takes a lot of extra power to cause marginal planing.

In heavy winds most people try to avoid going straight down wind and reach, then gybe and reach back. Steering sensitivity is critical to keeping the boat at top speed. Letting the boat heel causes hull and rudder drag when not corrected soon enough. Watch the wind on the water and waves to anticipate hiking or steering changes. Avoid sailing by-the-lee by watching the shroud telltales or masthead fly. If you feel gybing is too dangerous, be very cautious about rounding on to a beat tack. The critical part is before you get around far enough luff sails. Turn slowly in a lull and move weight to windward to counter new side wind pressures.

Tuning and balance

Since sails are stalled on a run most of the time, sail shape is not important. Sail area counts most so move the outhaul to the black band on the boom. Use normal boom vang tension to prevent too much twist at the top. Use a barber haul on the jib fairlead farther forward to prevent too much lift on the whisker pole causing excessive twist.

In some classes of boats, side forces to windward can be caused by twisting the top part of the mainsail to windward. This is very easily done if there are no shrouds to limit the boom. It is good practice to tie a stopper knot in the main sheet to prevent accidental windward forces. The centreboard should be almost up in light air on a run unless tacking downwind. Medium air requires $^1/_3$ down to maintain helm balance and steering control. Tilting the mast forward by shroud levers is allowed in some classes to improve downwind balance and speed.

Running in waves

Generally speaking, running is avoided in waves that cause constant attention to steering and no increase in speed.

In small lakes or with less wind, waves are difficult to cope with because the distance and time in which to manoeuver is short. The speed of the wave may or may not be an advantage when running.

The objective is to get on a wave and ride downwind with it as long as possible. The important things to consider then are the relative speed of the wave and the speed of the boat in that wind. Assume a wave is travelling at 9 knots and wind allows you to plane even faster if sails are driving. The best technique is to bear off down the face of the wave, move weight forward to keep the bow down until speed picks up and give the sails a pump. If you tend to go too fast, the bow will bury in the next wave and slow the boat and cause some danger of capsize. It is better to keep weight aft a little as in planing, luff sails just enough to match the wave speed and steer carefully to avoid tilting the boat by centrifugal force.

If the wave is travelling too slow and is too small to ride on, You must negotiate each wave as follows. Try to get a push from the wave as you sail down it with weight aft. Head up a little across the trough with weight still aft. As you head up the other side, bear away more squarely with the wave. When on top lean or slide forward to tilt the boat down the face again. It takes a lot of concentration but becomes easy with practice.

The other situation which is common on small lakes, is having waves too shallow and short to ride and not quite enough wind to keep up to the waves. In a marginal situation, the odd wave will be large enough to catch a ride on. Looking aft you must pick a wave, slide forward to get the bow down, as the stern is lifted the wave will push it forward. At the same time, one or two pumps on the sail may give the extra force to accelerate the boat to wave speed. Keep weight forward while riding it and trim to suit the apparent wind. When racing, be careful that pumping is limited to that allowed by rule 60 in the Yacht Racing rules.

If you have been reaching across the waves at an angle to improve boat speed you may have to gybe to return to a downwind destination.

Sailing in light air

There are two distinct categories of light air. Generally, between 4 and 8 knots, ripples on the water are visible to tell you where the wind is from. The sails fill, telltales work, and the helm responds because you can trim and get enough boat speed. The other category is called a drifter. In the range from 0-3 knots, the water is glassy and wind direction is difficult to determine. Many sailors and racers assume there is no wind and get bored and often move backwards.

The most important factor in any light air is to detect where the wind is from and trim to suit immediately. Look at the shore and the clouds and figure out where a thermal or geographic effect should encourage some breeze.

Sail shape in a 4 to 8 knot breeze requires more draft than a drifter once acceleration is established. How high you can point depends a lot on how smooth the water is. Some twist is required because the wind is stronger near the top than the foot of the sail, changing the apparent wind angle. Keep weight forward to improve weather helm and reduce wetted surface at the stern.

Some classes prefer a 10° angle of heel, others none. Steering must be gentle to avoid rudder turbulence.

In a drifter, a whole new approach to sailing is required. The following factors become important:

(1) Look for signs that indicate wind direction, shore smoke, other boats. Cigarette smoke works well when held to contrast against dark background.

(2) Use light shroud telltales. Very light jib yarn ticklers are most important and an extended piece of yarn at the mast head.

(3) Heel the boat to leeward to let the weight of cloth sag and shape sails. Lighter sail cloth fills better too.

(4) Keep very still, move slowly, don't spill wind from sails.

(5) Make sails flat by the outhaul, release cunningham and all luff tension. Flat sails 1/20 ratio maintain flow better.

(6) Move the mainsheet traveller to windward, ease vang to avoid a leech curving to windward.

(7) Shape the jib by hand holding clew to trim and control fullness and slot at leech.

(8) Sit forward bow down, stern out, minimum wetted surface.

(9) Centreboard must be down and forward for weather helm.

(10) Friction of hull and centreboard is relatively the biggest factor slowing the boat. Smooth the hull and leading edges of centreboard and rudder.

(11) Keep the boat moving and use momentum to carry through bald spots.

(12) Check that the boat is not moving backwards or is stopped. Wind often changes 180°.

(13) Keep air clear. Disturbances affect air for several boat lengths or diverts air over or around the boat and sails.

(14) Use spinnaker only if it fills properly, otherwise remove it.

(15) Be sure to rolltack, otherwise tacking can stop a boat completely.

4
SPINNAKER

Description of the spinnaker and its gear

The spinnaker is made of very strong, light, nylon material capable of bias stretch. Its light weight allows it to fill in very light air and lift to assume the design shape as well as pack easily into a small space. The shape is symmetrical on each side and curved from a vertical front lower half to a more horizontal shape at the top. When set properly, it gives the bow of the boat lift to counteract the tendency of the mainsail to bury the bow on a run.

The sail tends to stall on a dead run, so it only adds area. When reaching, the air flows from the luff around to the leech and generates more power. A specially designed reacher or flatter one can be used for close reaching when wind is a little lighter. When trimming the spinnaker, the shape can be controlled somewhat to influence the angle of the driving force and reduce backwinding on the mainsail.

The spinnaker pole is set on the mast to extend the luff five or more feet out to pick up as much wind as possible. The pole is always on the side opposite the boom. It has fittings at both ends that are identical, to allow gybing the sail to the opposite side when the mainsail is gybed. It is also fitted with a tripline below to release the clip remotely and a means of clipping an uphaul (topping lift) to carry the weight and to position it at the right height. A downhaul or line from the pole centre to the mast at deck level prevents it lifting too much.

The head of the spinnaker is hoisted up the mast above the forestay. The whole sail is rigged completely outside of shrouds and forestay, free to move from one side to the other when gybed. Identical sheets, called guy and sheet, are attached to the tack and clew cringles by clips on the sheets. These control the position and trim of the sail from the crew position. Each one is led aft to the side deck blocks nearer the transom and forward through a fairlead and jamb cleat. The position should be chosen to make it convenient to jamb by either helmsman or crew. Sometimes the two sheets are one-piece continuing across the boat near the thwart to make sure one does not pull loose and fly out of reach. Halyard and sheets should be of braided line, less likely to twist than layed line. The halyard runs through a block above the forestay, down to the foot of the mast, and aft to a jam cleat on the centreboard trunk, handy to the helmsman. The halyard has a swivel-type brummel hook to attach to a hook on the head cringle to discourage twisting of the head.

A reaching hook located just forward and outboard of the shrouds holds the end of the pole down when the guy is hooked into it. Perhaps the most important and least expensive detail is a piece of wool on each shroud to read the apparent wind direction at all times.

Shore training

You must first be familiar with the names of parts shown and how to prepare, hoist, fly, gybe and douse a spinnaker with the least complication. If we set the boat on the grass or sand facing downwind or even in shallow water facing downwind we can practise techniques. If you go out on the water first to practise you will spend most of your time beating back up wind to try again. Shore training is much faster and less complicated. Do not use a mainsail or jib the first time, but the boom supported by the main halyard should be used.

Pack the spinnaker in a turtle ready for hoisting. Use a basket, bag or carton with 2 corners notched to keep the 2 corners of the spinnaker separate. Lay the spinnaker out to identify the inside of the tack, clew and head and to keep them separate. The port reinforcement around the cringle and up the vertical binding is red, the starboard side green. Look for a different colour for the head. Pack to avoid twists when hoisting. Place one clew hanging out of the appropriate corner of the turtle. Run the hand along the foot and leave the other clew hanging out on its corner. Put the foot of the spinnaker in the turtle first, then as you run one hand up both leeches, pack the body of the spinnaker in so that the leeches will separate when pulled. When you reach the head, lay it forward opposite to the first two corners. Provide shock cord over the turtle to prevent it blowing out.

Rigging

The key to successful hoisting is packing and rigging the sheets outside of the shrouds and forestay. It is usually better to hoist in the lee of the mainsail so the halyard, sheet and guy must be led to the lee side and under the jib sheets. The turtle must be either on the lee side or in the middle. Use the following steps:

(1) Lead the guy outside the windward shroud and forestay and clip to the tack after passing under the jib sheets.

(2) Lead the sheet outside the other shroud, under the jib sheets and to the clew.

(3) Clip the halyard which is led down from a block to the head cringle after passing under the jib sheets or foot of the jib.

(4) Clip the spinnaker pole to the mast and support with the uphaul/downhaul so that the pole is about level with the water. Have open side of end fitting down.

(5) Holding the guy in one hand, use the pole trip line to clip the pole end to the guy and let it slide forward to the forestay.

Hoisting

The skipper stands, one foot either side of the centreline, facing forward and steering with the tiller between the knees. He holds the halyard ready.

The crew holds the sheet in one hand, the guy in the other facing forward.

(1) On signal, the skipper quickly hoists the spinnaker almost to the top with both hands and cleats it.

(2) At the same time the crew pulls both sheet and guy to separate the leeches and watches the sail fill right to the top.

(3) As soon as the sail begins to fill, the crew pulls the guy until the pole comes back almost in line with the boom or square with the apparent wind. This must be adjusted later.

(4) Trim the sheet until there is no tendency to curl at the luff. Note: with the mainsail blocking the wind, filling the sail will be slower. Try on shore with mainsail up.

(5) Adjust sheet and guy forward a little to move the sail

forward. This can also be adjusted by the distance of the head from the mast on the halyard. This distance is normally a few inches to a foot from mast to head.

A spinnaker can also be hoisted on a run on the windward side. Be sure to rig halyard and sheet around the forestay, and under the jib sheet. A very fast method used by crews of boats with small spinnakers is quite effective. The spinnaker is rigged on the windward side of the forestay. It can be packed into a plastic bottle with the bottom cut off and the handle tied to a line attached to the boat. Sheet and guy are adjusted to their normal position for flying the spinnaker. Each corner is left hanging out of the bottle a few feet.

When the skipper has almost hoisted the halyard, the crew throws the spinnaker in a tight bundle or bottle upwards and forward. The bottle flies ahead releasing the spinnaker and it opens and fills. The timing of hoisting and throwing is very important to prevent an hourglass or the sail blowing against the forestay and filling on both sides of it. If the plastic bottle was used, it falls in the water and is removed by its line as soon as the sail is flying properly,

Trimming the spinnaker on a run

The objectives are:

(1) To get maximum area presented to the wind beside the mainsail.

(2) To set the pole approximately at right angles to the apparent wind and cleat.

(3) To adjust the sheet to prevent collapse or stall and not restrict area between the leech and the mainsail.

(4) To steer so that apparent wind changes do not affect the setting of the guy, unless it takes you in the wrong direction.

It is the crew's job to hold sheet uncleated and guy cleated when set. They must watch heeling angle and spinnaker luff constantly. A slight curl of the luff on a run will not reduce area noticeably, but it does prove to skipper and crew that the leading part of the spinnaker is riot stalled and flow around the lee side is maximum. Continually ease the sheet slowly to the point of curling the luff and trim again quickly.

A full cut spinnaker is more stable when running than a flatter reaching cut. There is less side to side oscillation. Normally the jib should be rolled or lowered to prevent interference with flow of air around the spinnaker, after it is flying.

Trimming the spinnaker on a reach

The objective is to get more speed than with out the spinnaker. A genoa, on a planing beam reach, is normally faster than a spinnaker. The problem is that side forces are so great that the centreboard must be fully down to prevent leeway and the helmsman must bear away farther to prevent heeling. In each type of boat and speed of wind, the highest point of sail must be determined for the design of spinnaker used.

The technique is much the same as running but the crew must not only hike or trapeze, but at the same time, with guy cleated, trim accurately and prevent easy collapse. The point of best trim is when the following conditions are met:

(1) No stalling at the luff for maximum driving force.

(2) No curl at the luff maintain close to collapse

(3) Straight luff line in the direction facing it along the pole. It is controlled by pole height at the tack. It should be lower than on a run.

(4) The helmsman must steer accurately to control angle of heel by bearing off in gusts. He must try to steer to changes in apparent wind direction to avoid changing the pole setting too often.

(5) If the luff begins to collapse and the trim of the sheet cannot correct it, the helmsman must bear off and the crew must release the guy to reestablish flow, then trim the guy. Consider the guy as coarse adjustment and the sheet as fine adjustment.

Reaction to heeling gusts on a reach

The same rule applies as for reaching. Bear off in puffs to sail the boat under the heeling sail. If it is too late and you cannot bear off, ease the sheet to ease the pressure, then as the boat comes more upright, bear away and trim the sheet. When shore training, bearing away is accomplished by swinging the stern to windward.

Now that you have experimented with hoisting and trimming ashore, try dousing so that the hoisting can be perfected on shore. Try hoisting the mainsail to simulate true conditions. The jib should be hoisted before dousing the spinnaker.

Dousing a spinnaker

This requires careful teamwork to avoid getting the guy or spinnaker in the water and so that the spinnaker can be packed ready for hoisting. The main point to remember is that a sail held in the wind by the leech only, will stream out if the guy is released. If both leech and luff are pulled together it fills again. The same point applies if it gets in the water. It will suddenly stream aft under a moving boat and must not be restricted at two edges or it will fill and tear. Follow this procedure:

(1) Steer straight downwind if possible and especially if the wind is strong.

(2) Skipper holds halyard and guy, crew stands ready under the boom with sheet in hand.

(3) Release guy through pole end and let luff blow to leeward.

(4) Crew pulls sheet and pulls down and in on foot, packing it in turtle.

(5) Skipper releases halyard but maintains slight tension on it to keep wind from blowing it out and into the water in front of the boat.

(6) Keep two leeches separate and be sure the three corners are left out and separate.

Hoisting on a reach

This is basically the same as downwind hoisting behind the main with the pole set o the guy not at the tack. Let the pole rest against the forestay to begin. Drop centerboar ¾ down.

(1) Skipper hoists main quickly, both hands, and cleats.

(2) Crew pulls on both guy and sheet to separate the leeches.

(3) Crew pulls guy to the pole fitting and moves the pole off the forestay until the sail starts to fill, then trims the sheet to fully fill the sail and eases again.

(4) The skipper is ready to hike the boat to keep it flat. The key is tension on the sheet.

(5) Sheet the main to open a good slot between clew and aft side of main.

Gybing the spinnaker on a run

Now that the mechanics of getting it up and down are Understood, exchange places with skipper and crew and work out timing and signals by practice until it comes easy and almost automatic. Try gybing the spinnaker before trying the techniques on the water. Start with the boat on a run.

(1) Gybe the boom. Crew can lean backwards on the new windward side facing aft, grabbing the pole and trip line, depending on the particular boat.

(2) Crew quickly detaches the pole from the mast and moves it to windward.

(3) Clip pole on new guy and slide the fitting to the tack.

(4) Unclip pole from old guy and clip on the mast.

(5) Trim guy and sheet to suit.

The skipper must steer carefully to try to keep air in the sail. The crew must work quickly but without rocking the boat.

Solving difficulties

Some of the problems may not arise until on the water or until the wind gets stronger. The worst is probably running over and tearing the spinnaker. A broach and capsize can be impossible to prevent if action is not taken soon enough. Teamwork and controlled heeling are very important. Both helmsman and crew must be constantly aware of windshifts, gusts and tendency of the spinnaker to collapse if not trimmed properly.

(1) Hoisting will not work if the halyard happened to pass over one of the jib sheets. Pull the jib to the other side before connecting halyard and sheets under jib sheet.

(2) Dousing must be controlled. If the skipper lets go of the halyard, the spinnaker may end up under the boat.

(3) An hour glass when hoisting is simply the top part being twisted around and filling above the twist. To prevent it, be sure to pack it without a twist, and use braided halyard. The crew should open leech and luff while maintaining some tension on them as it goes up. To correct, an hour glass, put tension on the leeches, lower the head 3 feet and try to collapse the bottom and spin the top-half in the hands. It is seldom more than 180° out of position. If this does not work, lower the spinnaker and unwind it.

(4) The jib may be used at the same time as the spinnaker or rolled up. When used it must not interfere with the flow on the windward side of the spinnaker or power is lost. Ease the sheet to open the slot between spinnaker and jib.

(5) Improper trimming of a sheet on a run can cause the main driving force to act to windward and rolling side to side. Trim the sheet to make the force act straight forward.

(6) If both sheet and guy are streaming downwind, head up to a close reach until they stream against the lee side of the mainsail to retrieve them. Bear away and lower in the usual way.

(7) If in doubt whether to use a spinnaker on a beam reach or not, don't, especially in planing winds. If the reach is broad enough to shelter the jib behind the mainsail, use the spinnaker.

(8) The crew should use leather faced, fingerless gloves to avoid burns and blisters from the guy and sheet material.

(9) If the spinnaker collapses on a run it could be too far behind the mainsail or trimmed with too much curl.

The launcher

This device is built in boats that have a forestay attached aft of the bow, far enough to allow room for the opening ahead of it. Some smaller designs even have the opening located aft of the forestay and to one side of the centreline. Its greatest advantage is the ease of hoisting and dousing with only halyard sheets and pole to worry about. Halyards and sheets are attached all the time.

The first part of the sail to enter the chute opening is the patch just below the centre. It is attached to the spinnaker halyard tail end.

Spring-pole technique

A new type of spinnaker pole used in reaching simplifies hoisting and dousing when you go around a triangular course. The equipment and method of rigging is a little different:

(1) The spinnaker pole is not the same at both ends. One end fits only on the mast, the other end fits on either side on the guy.

(2) The uphaul is adjustable from the cockpit and is always connected,

(3) The forward guy acts as a downhaul to the foredeck and is adjustable for different pole heights and as it swings, it is always connected even when stowed.

(4) The mast end of the pole is fastened to long shock cord on the boom which pulls it into a slot on the boom for storage.

(5) Gybing is done by releasing the uphaul from its cleat and doing a dip-pole gybe. Release the pole from the guy, and when the boom has been gybed, connect the same end to the new guy after dipping it down past the forestay.

(6) Dousing is simply done by disconnecting the pole from both the mast and the guy and letting the shock cord pull the pole along the boom. The forward guy and uphaul do not need to be removed when it is stored there.

5

FITNESS FOR SAILING

Recreational sailing requires a level of fitness that is consistent with the goal of anyone who wants to feel good, be healthy and self-confident. It's a great feeling to stay young and flexible throughout a lifetime.

Hiking-out for long periods, self-rescue and trailering can be very tiring for a person not strong enough or out of shape. To perform these tasks easily and not feel exhausted, a person needs to build strength in specific areas of the body and develop stamina. Flexibility for the twisting and bending, and good balance in a boat are essential. Fitness makes sailing more invigorating and enjoyable. It requires only an average of 3% of your waking hours to maintain a reasonable level of fitness. The cost of joining a fitness club or providing your own facilities can be less than one day in the hospital. The investment in time need only be 2 or 3 hours a week to keep fit.

This section does not deal with advanced level of fitness suitable for top level international sailing competition. It does cover the fundamentals of exercise and a variety of methods I have found helpful in preparing for active club-racing and exciting sailing. Sailing is a good reason to keep fit year round. The problem, however, is that only 5% of those that decide to start a program continue on a permanent basis.

The hardest part of a successful program is to stick to it until it becomes a habit you would hate to live without. Many people give up and lose the benefits for the following reasons:

(1) Some do not understand the fundamentals of exercise well enough to start and develop a suitable personal program that is self-satisfying enough to continue.

(2) Some get bored before they begin to feel the benefits. The first three months is the hardest if you are out of shape.

(3) Some are so keen to reach a goal, they try too hard and too fast, get overtired, injure themselves, feel discouraged and give up.

(4) Some do not budget regular and specific times each week for exercise. It must become a habit that is part of living, like eating and sleeping. It's never too late to start and becomes increasingly important.

(5) Some need group incentive or a skilled instructor to guide them. You need the will-power to start and also some push or encouragement from friends or family. Continue at a level of exertion that is beneficial.

In any fitness program, the following feelings are usually experienced: (i) during a workout the physical and menta effort generates feelings of pleasure, pain and exhaustion. (ii) after a hard workout there may be a feeling of exhaustion for a few minutes or even half an hour until by-products are removed from the blood. (iii) for about 48 hours after a good workout there will be a feeling of relaxation, vibrant good health and well being.

How to start a personal program

There are a variety of ways that will achieve a general fitness level. Whatever program you choose, it must suit your own needs, desires and short and long-term goals. Investigate the best time and facilities, and your present physical condition. Here are some suggestions:

(1) Have a complete medical checkup if you have been relatively inactive physically. This will not prevent problems, but it will identify for you areas of risk or weaknesses that increased physical exercise could reveal. A blood test will make it possible to correct any condition caused by improper diet. To supply enough energy, you will need to eat a proper balance of protein, minerals, carbohydrates, fat and sugar.

So called "junk food" habits lack the recommended 65% of fruit and vegetables to aid digestion. People over 30 should be checked for cardiac problems and high blood pressure.

(2) Take physical tests to find out your level of endurance, strength and flexibility. Endurance is associated with heart and lung efficiency. A simple test you can do at home as a measure of your efficiency is as follows: It is based on your system's ability to return to resting heart rate after exercise. Rest for 15 minutes and using a watch and your fingers beside your adam's apple, record your 10 second resting rate. It may be 10 to 12 beats. Now step up on a 16" high box, then step down using alternate feet 24 times in one minute. Take a 10 second test immediately, then again after one minute. Your heart rate will increase then slow down again. Compare the final reading 1 minute and 10 seconds after you stopped, with your starting rate. The difference in beats is a measure of your stamina

condition to compare with the following: 0 excellent, 1-2 good, 3-4 fair, 5-6 poor. Compare results with those after 2 months conditioning.

For sailing, you should be able to do 30 (bent knee) situps and 30 half knee-bends at least. The stomach and leg endurance exercise helps for normal hiking-out. Flexibility of the whole body, especially arms, legs and ankles is important for dinghy sailing. Any program should include both endurance and flexibility exercise.

(3) Investigate what facilities are available for year-round activities such as swimming, running and gym. Is there a fitness class available that you can regularly attend? Are you interested in general muscle fitness and strength improvement only, or also flexibility and cardio-vascular (heart, lung and muscle) efficiency?

(4) It is not advisable to run on concrete or frozen ground near the beginning of a program. It may cause enough shock effect on feet, ankles, knees or back to defeat the purpose of exercise or delay progress. Buy top-quality cushion-soled shoes with rounded heel and toe to absorb the shock. Shoes can make a big difference in how far you can run easily and how you feel right after, or the next day. Yoga exercises for flexibility of feet and ankles, and a suitable warm up may be the secret to real improvement.

(5) Do not expect immediate results. The first three months is the hardest. Do not overdo it, thereby delaying progress by exhaustion or injury, A proper, gradual and progressive program, suited to your condition, will improve appetite and confidence. It

may take 1 to 3 years to reach your fitness goal depending partly on your age.

(6) Do not exercise for 2 to 3 hours after a meal. Digestion takes a lot of blood circulation and competes with your exercises for heart and lung capacity. It could cause pains or feelings of faintness.

(7) Do not try to compete with other members of a fitness class. Set your own progressive, challenging, but sensible limits. How you feel half an hour after is a guide. Warm up before doing flexibility stretching to avoid a muscle injury. Always stretch slowly and progress a little each time, but never beyond mild pain, and never bounce.

(8) Two months before sailing season, concentrate more on specific exercises to condition legs, arms and stomach muscles for hiking endurance.

(9) Learn enough about fundamentals of exercise physiology to set and monitor your own program to get a training effect and a good relaxed feeling afterwards.

Fundamentals of exercise physiology

The body will try to develop to meet the physical demands put on it, provided there is proper food and rest. The heart muscle expands its capacity, the lungs become more efficient and muscles grow and stretch to become stronger and more flexible. Without exercise, unused muscles and tissue become weaker, softer, age faster and are unable to meet increased demands such as those required in active sailing. The heart pumps less bood and has to increase speed to keep up with small extra demands.

Work requires energy. The energy comes from food.

The food forms chemicals which are carried in the blood and stored in the muscles.

When signalled to do work, the muscle contracts, its length shortens and pulls on the bones attached to its two ends. When the bones are moved against a load, such as lifting, work is done.

Work lasting only a few seconds uses energy stored in the muscle. As the length of work time increases, the need for oxygen increases, and the need to get rid of wastes such as carbon dioxide and lactic acid increases. The blood circulation system must speed up. The heart rate increases and pumps more blood. The lungs are fully utilized to get more oxygen to the blood and expel wastes by rapid and deeper breathing.

Strength: Exercise of the muscles causes fibres to increase in size not in number. Blood capillories, however, can be increased in size, number and condition by endurance training over long periods of time. If the heart and lungs can supply the oxygen, the muscle will then have both more strength and more endurance. As fitness improves, more work or exercise can be done with less effort, at a lower heart rate and with less gasping for air.

Heart-rate recovery, after one to five minutes is faster, which shows up in feeling good sooner after stopping. Muscle tone and resistance to bruises improves, which is good news for crews who tend to suffer more bruises than skippers.

Endurance: The fundamental of improving endurance fitness effectively is to stress muscles, heart and lungs well beyond normal activity level for short periods two or three times a week. In the period after exercise, new tissue will grow, given proper food and rest. The ability to meet this extra challenge or stress will improve each time.

Work on exercise that causes heart beat increase such as running, swimming, cycling perhaps only a total of 35 minutes a week minimum for results. The heart rate should be increased for 6 to 12 minutes each time to 120 beats per minute or nearly double normal resting rate. A training effect will occur when done progressively and not overdone. You should not be overtired half an hour after stopping. Endurance for specific muscles require regular increases in reptitions of stressing of those muscles. This improves the conditioning and tone to transport blood and remove wastes more efficiently.

Flexibility: An important aspect of fitness is flexibility. Each muscle is flexible because it shortens while being flexed, returns to normal when relaxed, but when stretched reaches a limit of length. When not stretched to its limit for a long time, it gradually shortens and limits bone movement a little. When muscles are unused, mobility, strength and agility are reduced. A young body is flexible and is usually active enough to maintain that flexibility. If arms, legs, torso, feet, ankles, knees, hands, neck and back are not stretched and twisted on a fairly regular basis, preferably to their limit, a person becomes stiffer, more awkward and lacks balance. A muscle injury is more likely to occur in the form of a pulled muscle when not conditioned. General health eventually deteriorates.

To increase flexibility, once lost, regular stretching and twisting of as many muscles as possible three times a week is necessary. Stretching should be followed by relaxing and deep breathing to achieve maximum removal of waste products.

General fitness improvement

Progress can be seen by the ability to do more work or run faster or farther with less effort, with a lower resting and working heart beat rate. It will return to normal in less time. A rule of thumb for maximum safe heart rate is 200 per minute minus age, while exercising. Resting rate will become 10 to 15 beats a minute lower after a successful long term program than before you started. It tends to be much lower in athletes, but the actual rate is not as significant as the improvement. Women have a slightly higher normal rate than men.

Understanding the above fundamentals makes it much easier to develop and monitor your own program and avoid discouraging set backs.

Warm-up: A car that has been warmed up works more efficiently. Warm up of the body also helps it perform better. There is less feeling of stiffness, more strength available and less chance of injury with unusual stress. We know how weak muscles become when very cold. Warm-up gets the blood circulating to the muscles for more energy, oxygen and strength. When sailing or exercising, avoid a cold start. In cold weather, keep the muscles warm for hiking and they will perform better with less chance of injury or stiffness. It is also important after strenuous exercise to taper off or slow down at the end.

A pulled muscle is painful when used and does not heal unless rested. It may take days or many weeks to heal a muscle injury and your activity and exercise may have to be curtailed. If serious or involving flexibility, you may need physiotheraphy.

Specific types of programs for sailing

Everyone is different and some have different reasons for

fitness than others. Most people need to improve flexibility, balance, and hiking-out endurance for sailing. Most crews need specific strength and muscle tone improvements as well.

For hiking endurance there are two areas that suffer the most if unfit. The stomach muscles are used a lot and can be improved by situps and large numbers of repetitions on a homemade hiking bench. Most people that race have one of sorts that simulates the hiking position. The other muscles that pain when hiking a lot are those on the front of the thighs above the knees. These require more strength and specific repetitions on the hiking bench for endurance. An exercise for both skiers and sailors to improve these muscles is half knee bends requiring little time and no equipment. Try running up many flights of stairs for good endurance exercise.

The back muscles are not used much when hiking, but should be strengthened by tension exercises. For example, lie on the stomach and lift head, shoulders and arms, increasing the number of repetitions each workout. A weak back should be given only specific exercise a doctor should prescribe. The biggest danger to backs is when lifting a boat in an awkward position or without a straight back. Use the legs to take the load.

Racing dinghy and some racing keel-boat sailors use a hanging type of hiking technique, sometimes called superhiking. It is more demanding of lower legs until you get used to it, but can be maintained for much longer periods. Superhiking consists of getting the body farther out so the knees are over or outside the gunwale and you can then sit on the outside of the hull. It requires hiking straps adjusted up to deck level and farther from the centreline. There is more strain on the lower legs and less on the upper legs and stomach. The problem when not conditioned for it, is getting back in. You must straighten out and slide in. You or your crew will need either excellent muscle tone or sponge rubber pads on the back of the legs.

Jogging and running: Jogging might best be described as a lower form of running, or moderate running and then walking to avoid fatigue and to allow a longer time for training without fatique. Walking is a good way to start jogging, then you can progress to jogging and running

Cooper's test is based on how far you can run or walk in 12 minutes. This will classify your condition and allow for age. Always warm up and cool down by walking at any level. Running is an efficient way to increase heart rate for training and most people find it quite enjoyable. For recreational sailing you should progress to running a mile in 8 minutes or less.

Cooper's Aerobic charts for various activities and specific ages and fitness categories will be helpful in developing a program for endurance fitness. Breathe in through the nose, out through the mouth. If any chest tightness or pains are felt, just walk. You may be pushing too hard or running too soon after a meal. Breathe deeply to improve oxygen intake. Take pulse rate immediately after stopping for 10 seconds and multiply by 6. It should fall rapidly in the first minute when condition improves.

Calisthenics: These can be done in a fitness class or at home using the Armed Forces fitness books XBX or 5BX for women or men. There are categories for age and ability which provide for gradual progress. The time limit suggested is important to get full benefit. Go from one exercise to the other. If you are too winded or feel faint, jog on the spot and breathe normally until you recover.

Breathing deeply for too long or hyperventilation can also cause a faint feeling.

There are dozens of exercises available that work on various parts of the body. It is a good idea to switch from one type to another rather than do all push-ups or arm exercises at one time. Alternate from one part of the body to another so you will not get fatigued and discouraged. A set of aerobic exercises can alternate from astride jumps to ski jumps to push-ups and back to astride jumps to keep the heart rate up above 120. Stretching exercises should be done slowly and are a good way to cool off.

If you take part in a fitness class, it is wise to pace yourself to the level which challenges, but does not exhaust you. You should not compete with the others when not ready. If you have stiffness the next day, it indicates you stressed muscles until there was oxygen debt and your circulation system needs further development to provide enough oxygen and carry away waste. A hot bath or sauna after exercise will help relax you and avoid stiffness. Warm-down helps avoid stiffness.

Weight training for strength: Using weights to increase specific muscle strength is normally only needed by some competitive sailors.

Caution is advised here to avoid straining muscles. The basic procedure is simple. Warm up first, and select a weight that challenges you for 6 repetitions, rest, and do another set of 6. The next work out, 2 or 3 days later, you should increase one repetition per set. When you can do 2 sets of 15 repetitions, increase the weight and start again with 6 repetitions. A workout will consist of a number of different exercises for each different muscle.

This requires professional guidance such as a fitness club to gain maximum benefits.

It is important to chart each exercise, weight and number of repetitions to be done at each session and check off when done. Without this record, the training effect may be lost if you forget any detail. For hiking practice, a hiking bench is fine for many repetitions for stamina, but to strengthen the thigh and stomach muscles, a weight will have to be raised by the ankles or the muscles loaded in some way. Muscles must be used or they become weaker. If the order of a program is reversed, you may find exercises done first seem easier because you are not tired. The same order of exercise is best for a progressive loading effect.

Be sure to warm up before lifting weights and combine the program with a general fitness program for best results. Never stress muscles beyond mild pain and do it slowly.

Gaining or losing weight: If you wish to gain weight as part of your fitness program for sailing, you must include muscle building. It is also necessary to increase your appetite by exercise and eat more calories. Although increasing intake of fat and sugar will put on weight, it is not a healthy approach, eat more whole wheat products, and dried fruits.

You may be interested in losing weight for racing and to look and feel better. This means losing fat. Remember that muscle weighs a little more than fat, so weight loss may be small at first in a fitness program.

Surplus fat cannot be removed in specific areas nor by diet or exercise alone. There must be a reduction in calorie intake below the amount normally required. In addition, the excess fat must be burned off by exercise.

This point is very important, as many programs of losing weight have failed because the exercise was not maintained for at least 20 minutes each time to immobilize the fat. In some cases, endurance is poor so that oxygen cannot be carried to the muscles to combine with the fat to oxidize it. A program would then have to develop enough fitness, then continue diet and suitable exercise that demands energy for longer periods. The program must be long term and crash diets are not successful for long, or healthy.

Isometrics: Isometrics is the name given to a technique for improving muscle strength at a specific joint angle by stressing the muscle without movement. If, for example, you press both hands together with at least 2/3 of your maximum strength for 6 seconds, there will be a training effect on the muscles stressed.

This can be done by developing specific muscles used for sailing. Each exercise should be done 3 times a day for 8 weeks to notice improvement. It takes no equipment and little time. Instead of lifting a weight 6 to 15 times with a rope and pulley to simulate a sheet, you can pull in the same direction much harder to force the same muscles to grow to meet the challenge.

Isometrics should be only used in conjunction with a general conditioning program.

Conditioning by sailing: It is true that for the level of fitness required for recreational sailing, it may be possible, if you sail three times a week in good winds, to stay in shape for most situations. If winds have been light, or you do not sail regularly, some endurance program should be maintained in the sailing season, part of the time.

Crewing

To become a good crew it requires training and practice to do the jobs effectively. Also good communication at a level the crew can understand. It also requires a desire to be a good crew and make the skipper appreciate those skills. Training must include perfecting all the maneouvers of tacking, gybing, trimming, adjusting weight and sail shape as required. In order to communicate with the crew, the skipper must know what sailing language the crew knows and practise signals they both understand. Later as they work better together, less talk and more instinctive reaction takes place. Much of the following will help most when racing.

The crew's point of view

Many crews get frustrated at first because the skipper seems to expect more than he has a right to. The skipper either does not know the crew's limitations at that level or does not have enough crewing experience to understand the crew's problems. Most problems arise when racing because some skippers tend to get too upset about slight mistakes that cause losses. The crew may notice losses due to skipper mistakes or tactical errors that are quite significant, but they must be overlooked to maintain that most important positive attitude. They must encourage each other diplomatically.

Training

Crews often go along for a chance to sail or to learn sailing from a friend. A skipper cannot go sailing in most two-man boats without a crew so they need each other. A skipper should consider the following points when training a crew:

(1) Consider previous experience and physical condition.

(2) Adjust hiking straps to suit crew's size and type of hiking expected.

(3) Have a session to discuss sailing language and orders to be used when tacking, gybing, etc.

(4) Show the crew what adjustments are required and the easiest way to make them, considering crew strength.

(5) Have a practice session ashore and on the water, tacking again and again to work out problems, then gybing, using the whisker pole, spinnaker packing and flying, and use of the trapeze. Obviously the crew would need some previous experience or the training would have to be gradual. Practice sessions are far better than going into a race and fumbling through or taking a season to work out problems.

(6) Find out the crew's limitations and assign specific jobs. Review the timing of orders, for example the words "ready about" must be followed by a pause while the crew makes the sheet ready and determines which foot to move first. Give the signal "hard alee" and determine when the tiller will begin to move. A good crew keeps the jib driving as long as possible and does not let it act as a brake.

(7) Practise problem areas until the crew feels confident, at ease and begins to move instinctively.

(8) Review other duties such as looking out for rocks or other boats.

(9) Practise hiking together in a gust and show how flat you want the boat kept. This may reveal poor condition or uncomfortable hiking straps.

(10) Be sure the crew can handle the tiller in case you must make repairs or you fall overboard.

(11) Teach the crew to helm the boat so you can demonstrate and work out crew techniques and appreciate the crews problems.

(12) Agree on how each will avoid critical remarks and maintain a positive attitude in the boat.

(13) Discuss fitness programs that will bring both skipper and crew to a desired level for the type of sailing or racing you want to do. This approach to crew training will surely improve performance and enjoyment more rapidly.

Communication

This is the area of teamwork that is so important in sailing. If you give an order that is not consistent each time, the result will be frustrating to both. Always use the same term as practised. Timing varies with the wind and is so important in roll tacking or heavy air tacking and gybing for best results. The crew must hear your signal.

A crew must also communicate if not ready or if something is wrong. Constantly feed information to the skipper on details he may need such as: compass changes, wind change coming, other boats near or even when the skipper is not steering or trimming correctly for a moment. Most skippers appreciate this help and use what they need to decide the next move. Be sure the crew does not assume the skipper can see another boat on collision course, there is a considerable blind spot. The crew should discuss any problem that detracts from the enjoyment of the sport.

Importance of the crew

There are many times when the crew is really the most important member aboard. In light air, for example, the crew finds the wind direction, sets the jib to suit and makes the boat go. In heavy air, the trimming and adjustments a good crew makes or hiking precisely at the right moment can make a big difference in boat speed or keeping upright. Spinnaker flying requires greater skill by the crew in keeping the boat at full speed and the spinnaker from collapsing or getting fouled. When using a trapeze, the crew must be agile, fast and fit, but physically, it may be easier than hiking. It is certainly more effective. A racing skipper considers a good crew as just as big an asset as a good boat,

Trade places with the crew

If you want to know how to appreciate a crew's problems and learn how to improve conveniences and efficiency, try crewing in your own boat. You may find that some equipment is too awkward to use or what you've been expecting to be done is not practical. It may be a chance to demonstrate easier ways to fly a spinnaker or set a whisker pole. Usually the owner will make some changes or repairs as a result.

Some man/woman, skipper/crew combinations are very effective in racing because they have arranged for each to do the jobs they are best suited for. This may mean having the lighter woman steer, the heavier man hike and call the shot on tactics or whatever. Success always improves team spirit.

The crew is usually responsible for trimming the jib and spinnaker, adjusting the centreboard, boom vang, main and jib cunningham and the jib luff tension. Many of these lines can be led aft to the thwart where either one can do them. Keeping the boat flat, watching for other boats or obstructions and helping gybe the boom are also part of the crew's job. These jobs require a keen interest, good physical condition and practice to do well, especially if racing in more challenging classes. Most crews also share the job of rigging and maintaining the boat. When day sailing, the stress on fast easy adjustment for maximum boat speed is less important, so crew involvement will depend on the level of interest.

A skipper must always be in charge of and responsible for the crew and boat. A skipper, fortunate enough to have a good crew who knows when to hike, trims constantly on a reach, and keeps a positive attitude in the boat, is indeed fortunate.

6

SAILS

The sails are the most important part of any sailboat. What they are made of and how they are handled by the skipper, more than anything else, determine how well and how fast a boat will sail. Thus it is important that you learn something about the parts of sails, bow they are made, and how they are used.

Modern mainsails and jibs are made of Dacron, a man-made fiber, Up until the early 195o's, however, sails were made of finely woven Egyptian cotton. We can all be thankful for the discovery that Dacron cloth makes good sails, for it has solved a very serious problem—the need to "break in"' a new suit of sails. Cotton sails must be very carefully broken in. They stretch out of shape very easily and do not return to their original shape. Thus, if they are handled carelessly during breaking in, cotton sails can be ruined. They also shrink when they are wet, and are subject to, attack by mildew.

Dacron sails, on the other band, do not suffer to the same extent from any of these shortcomings. Dacron sailcloth is elastic. Thus when it is stretched out of shape it will spring back to its original shape when released, if it has not been subjected to excessive wind force. This allows the sailmaker to cut and sew sails exactly as he wants them. If he is good at his job, the finished sail will set just as he planned it on the drawing board. Dacron sails are not damaged by mildew, which will form on the sail surface. They are, however, affected by some of the chemicals that pollute the air around large cities. In addition, Dacron sails are affected by beat; a live ash from a cigarette or pipe will melt a bole instantly.

As sturdy as Dacron sails are, they can be damaged in heavy weather. Not too long ago, while sailing a twenty-four-foot sloop on Long Island Sound, my family and I found ourselves sailing into the teeth of a northwest wind that was gusting to about thirty-five knots. If we hadn't had to get home, we would have been wise to pull into a sheltered harbor to wait the wind out. As it was, we had to tack some fifteen miles into that very strong wind. We furled the mainsail, and tacked using just the working jib until we were right off home port. At this point the waves were running six to eight feet, making it impossible to go forward to lower the jib. As a result, when we switched to power and beaded directly into the wind, the jib luffed, wildly, even though we tried to hold it tight with the sheet lines. This wild luffing caused the sail to tear in several places, showing that as tough as Dacron is, it can be damaged. Sailing in thirty-five-knot winds is not recommended, either. If we had it to do over again, we would head into that sheltered harbor and wait for the wind to go down, regardless of how important it was to get home.

To care for your mainsail properly, don't leave it furled on the boom for long periods of time, unless you protect it with a sail cover. It is much better to stow the main along with the jib in sail bags, or in a dry locker at the yacht club or at home. At the end of the season, if your sails don't require repairs by the sailmaker, you can store them yourself. Simply hose them down with fresh water, fold them neatly after they are dry, and stow them away in their bags in a dry, cool place. If salt has accumulated on the sail, it should be scrubbed off.

Mainsails

The mainsail is the principal driving sail on a fore-and-aft-rigged boat. Virtually all small sailboats in use today are fore-and-aft-rigged. They carry one of three types of mainsail: the *jib-headed, or* Marconi; the *gaff-headed;* or the *loose-footed.*

The type of mainsail you will most likely work with is the jib-headed. As the drawing shows, a jib-headed main is long, narrow, and triangular. But it is much more than a large piece of triangular sailcloth. The sail must have a curved shape when set in order for it to drive the boat properly. This curve is called the *draft* of the sail. For light winds, a sail should have a fairly deep draft. In heavy weather it is better for the sail to be flatter in shape. Dedicated racing skippers carry several suits of sails, with varying amounts of draft, to permit them to use the sail that best matches the wind conditions. On good mainsails, the deepest part of the curve of the draft is about one-third the distance from the mast going aft toward the leech. The curve then flattens out to a straight line as it approaches the trailing edge of the sail.

The drawing shows how the draft is produced in a sail. First, the strips of cloth that make up the sail are sewn together. Note how the seams are at right angles to the line of the leech. Then, when the sail is cut, the luff and the foot are cut along a curve, not on a straight line. The result, when the sail is bent on the straight mast and straight boom, is the draft of the sail. Because the mast and boom are straight, the excess cloth of the curved cuts along the luff and foot appear as the draft. To maintain proper draft, you can see that it is important to keep the mast and boom as straight as possible. This applies to the beginning sailor. Many experts, on the other hand, use a "bendy" rig to good advantage when racing. On a bendy rig, the mast and boom are deliberately bent out of the straight position.

A gaff-headed mainsail is quite different from the jib-headed main. It is a foursided (quadrilateral) sail with the top edge held aloft by a spar called a *gaff.* Gaff-headed sails are cut shorter on the luff and longer on the foot than jib-headed sails. One reason gaff-headed sails have lost popularity is difficulty of handling. They are heavier than jib-headed sails; the sail itself is much larger, and the gaff also must be hauled aloft, Such sails must be raised by two halyards—one at the peak and one at the throat. Under way, gaff-rigged boats do not sail to windward as efficiently as boats carrying jib-headed sails. Because of their very large sail area, however, gaff-rigged boats usually sail off the wind-reaching and running—much better than their sisters with jib-headed mainsails.

Loose-footed mainsails are similar in shape to jib-headed mains. The foot of the sail, however, is not attached to the boom. Instead, the sail is fastened to the end of the boom by a single line attached to the clew. The set of the sail can be changed by lengthening or shortening the line running from the clew to the end of the boom. The shorter the line, the flatter the sail. Loose-footed mains are usually found on smaller sailboats. For example, certain small dinghies rigged with the mast stepped well forward, and carrying a mainsail only, use the loose-footed mainsail.

Before moving on to the different types of jibs, let me point out that the parts of sails generally have the same names, even though the sails may be different, Thus, the leading edge of a sail is always the *luff,* and the trailing edge is always the *leech.* The lower edge is always called the foot, and the top corner the *head.* The tack is the lower corner at the front of the sail, and the *clew is* the lower corner at the trailing edge of the sail. There are slight exceptions to these terms on gaff-rigged mainsails and spinnakers. The drawing shows these exceptions for a gaff main. They will be pointed out for the spinnaker shortly.

Jibs

Old-timers called them staysails; today almost everyone calls them *jibs.* The jib is the single sail forward of the mast on a sloop. There are several different types of jib: the *working jib;* the so-called *genoa jib;* the *reaching jib,* or *ballooner;* the storm *jib;* and the *jib* topsail. The working jib and genoa jib are the most important as far as we are concerned. They are in constant use on practically all sailboats, and both will almost certainly be in use on the first sloop-rigged boat you step aboard.

The working jib is a triangular sail usually cut straight on the foot and on the leech. As mentioned, the jib is rigged forward of the mast. It fits within the triangle formed by the deck, the mast, and the jibstay. On most jibs, a strong but light cable called the *luff wire* is sewn into the luff of the sail. The luff wire ends in loops at the head and tack of the sail. Thus, when the jib is raised, it cannot be overstretched. Quite the contrary, many careless sailors fail to tighten the luff wire enough when they raise the jib. When this happens, the sail sags between the jib snaps along the luff, producing a kind of scalloped effect. The jib does not work well when set up this way, for it must be perfectly smooth from luff to leech for maximum efficiency. A good rule of thumb when raising the jib is to tighten the luff wire just enough to produce a slight slack in the jibstay. This will usually guarantee enough tension in the luff wire.

The jib has several important functions. Most

important, it creates a driving force, thus helping to push the boat through the water. In addition, when it is set properly with respect to the, mainsail, it enhances the driving force of the main. As you recall, it is the wind "slot effect" of a well-set jib that increases the drive of the main. The jib also smoothes the flow of the wind, and it assists in the steering of a sailboat by acting to balance the forces on the boat.

A taut luff wire guarantees that the jib will have its proper shape. But more important than that, if the jib is not set up properly the skipper loses one of his best indications that the boat is sailing correctly. When sheeted in properly, the jib will be quietly full at the luff, assuring the skipper that he is getting the best he can out of his sails. On the other hand, the luff of the jib may shiver gently, or even shake violently, depending upon how the sail is sheeted in with respect to the wind. As you gain experience at the helm, you will learn to make frequent checks of the luff of the jib. More than anything else, it will help you set the sails on your boat properly. People often bear the term "working sails" applied to the mainsail and a small jib, This term goes back to the days when fishing boats and other work boats were powered by sail alone. This combination of jib and mainsail was the easiest to handle on such boats, hence the term "working sails."

The genoa jib is a much larger sail, also triangular in shape. It gets its name from a similarity to a sail used by fishermen near the city of Genoa, Italy. As the drawing shows, genoa jibs have a very long foot; they overlap the mainsail, and must be sheeted way aft. As a result, they have to be set outside the shrouds. Because of their greater area, and because they form a longer and more definite slot between main and jib, genoa jibs supply more drive than working jibs. Almost all of the larger cruising type sailboats carry genoa jibs; many smaller boats do also. The genoa jib is used to obtain more speed when the wind is light enough to make the working jib ineffective. Genoas are primarily used for beating and for close reaching. They become quite difficult to handle when the wind is astern, although you will occasionally see a boat running before the wind with a small genoa jib set "wing-and-wing" with a mainsail.

As you can readily see, the enormous area of a genoa jib makes it difficult to handle. When filled with wind, such jibs pull so bard on the sheet line they must be sheeted in with the help of a winch, Winches, you recall, are simple wheel-and-axle devices that make it easier to pull in a heavy load. But this strong pull on the sheet line isn't the only problem the skipper and crew face when a genoa jib is in use. If through carelessness the skipper finds himself in too strong a wind for safe sailing, his boat may be in danger of capsizing. Wise skippers learn early in the game just how much wind their boats can take when a genoa is in use. The foolish sailors often get a sudden and violent dunking.

Coming about with a genoa jib on the boat is not as simple or quick as it is with a working jib. First, the clew of the sail must come forward past the shrouds and around the mast. While this is taking place, there is a danger that the sheet line or the sail itself will snag. Thus it is often necessary for a crew member to carry the clew forward around the mast. All of this means that the tack has to be performed much more slowly than with a working jib. It can't be done too slowly, though, or the boat may go into "irons"—that is, the boat may stall and lose headway, with the sails luffing, halfway through the coming-about maneuver.

Look back at the diagram of a jib-headed mainsail

and note the extra sail area along the leech called the roach. The extra material of the roach adds drive to the sail when reaching or running before the wind. But the roach is apt to curl or flap if it isn't supported. This support is supplied by long, narrow slats called *battens*. Made of wood, plastic, or aluminium, battens are slipped into pockets sewn into the sail. Batten pockets should be one to two inches longer than the battens they hold. In addition to use on mainsails, battens are often used on working jibs. Their effect once again is to support and smooth the trailing edge of the sail. If battens are made and fitted to a sail correctly, they will bend to the shape of the sail and form a smooth curve. This allows the wind to flow over the sail with no interruption. A batten that is too stiff, however, forms a sharp bend in the sail, and obstructs the smooth flow of the wind.

You can save yourself a lot of trouble with broken and lost battens if you follow a few simple rules. Insert battens carefully to avoid tearing the pocket seams. When fully inserted, be sure the batten is either tied securely or locked into the pocket. It is also advisable to remove the battens when the sail is furled or packed away into a bag. A broken batten does little good and may poke through the sail. A batten that has flown out of its pocket, only to sink or float away from the boat, is also useless.

The spinnaker

Very few sights on the water can equal the *sheer beauty* of a sailboat running before the wind with its spinnaker set perfectly. If possible, an even more awe-inspiring sight is a fleet of competing cruising-class sailboats, all with their spinnakers set and lifting. Perhaps you've had the good fortune to witness such a racing fleet emerge from the horizon on, say, Long Island Sound, San Francisco Bay, or Lake Michigan. It's a sight to remember. Although the majority of sails are white, spinnakers are usually multicolored in a variety of different geometric designs, adding to the spectacle as the fleet passes by.

The modern spinnaker is used for reaching and for sailing before the wind. Spinnakers vary considerably in shape, depending on such factors as the design of the boat and the ideas of sailmakers and skippers. Thus, you may see long, narrow spinnakers, as well as round, egg, and bell-shaped ones. Because the sail is used a great deal in light winds, it is made from very light but very strong nylon fabric. If you've been observant, you've noticed that many spinnakers are dark in color at the top of the sail but light in color at the bottom. There's a reason for this. Some people feel that the dark fabric absorbs heat from the sun, and then warms the air beneath it inside the upper portion of the sail. Warm air, of course, rises. Thus, this warming effect gives greater lift to the sail, helping to bold it up where it belongs in very light winds.

Spinnakers are not easy to set, nor are they easy to control once they are flying. But more about this later. Look at the diagram of a spinnaker in position, The top corner of the sail is the *head* and the bottom edge, the foot. Unlike other sails, both side edges are called *leeches,* and both lower corners are called *clews. On* the windward side of the boat, opposite the mainsail, a *spinnaker boom* or *pole is* rigged from the mast to the clew of the sail. The corner of the sail the spinnaker pole is attached to is called the *tack,* but only while the pole is rigged this way. The side edge of the sail above the tack is then called the luff. Often, however, it is necessary to change the course of the boat, requiring that the mainsail and the spinnaker pole be shifted to the opposite side of the boat. This tactic is called *jibing the spinnaker.* It will be explained later. The important thing to note here is that when the spinnaker is jibed, the tack and luff of the sail also move over to the other side.

The spinnaker is controlled by several lines. It is raised by the spinnaker halyard and held in position by several other lines. The sheet line is attached to the loose, hanging corner of the sail, the clew. The other corner, the tack, is usually controlled by three separate lines. One of these, the topping lift, runs from the mast to the spinnaker pole. In addition, an *after* guy runs from the outer end of the spinnaker pole back to the cockpit, and a *forward* guy runs to the foredeck and then back to the cockpit. The topping lift and guy lines permit the crew to move the tack of the spinnaker up and down and forward and aft. To be effective, the spinnaker must be very carefully adjusted to the frequent wind shifts that seem to occur when a boat is sailing downwind. It takes a highly skilled and coordinated crew to do this job well.

Spinnakers, despite their great efficiency and beauty, can cause serious trouble at times. For example, because the nylon fabric used is very light, it may tear in heavy winds. More than one skipper, trying to make up lost time in a wind too heavy for a spinnaker, has watched in chagrin as the wind has torn the sail to shreds, The tattered fragment left at the masthead makes a fine, if very expensive, wind pennant. Sometimes, too, the spinnaker can fly out of control as it is being set or jibed. When this happens the sail usually wraps itself around the jibstay. Needless to say, it is very difficult to untangle this kind of snarl-up. Smart skippers try to prevent this problem by rigging a harness between the jibstay and mast that serves to block the spinnaker as it begins to curl around the jibstay. It helps also to have a crew that knows what it is doing. Beautiful, efficient, but tricky and full of surprises; this, in a nutshell, sums up the spinnaker.

7

RIGGING

The rigging used to support the mast is called standing rigging. As the drawing of one possible arrangement shows, the standing rigging consists of several different stays and shrouds. Shrouds support the mast at its sides, and stays support it fore and aft. Let's first consider the stays and what they accomplish. The rig shown is called a seven-eighths rig because the *jibstay* ends about seven-eighths of the distance up the mast. As you can see, it ties into the mast somewhat below the backward pull of the permanent *backstay.* On some boats you will see *running backstays* instead of a permanent backstay. When the boat is under sail, beating to windward, the pressure on the mainsail pulls the top of the mast aft. At the same time, the jib is pulling the mast forward at the point where the jibstay is tied in. You now see why the jumper struts and *jumper stays* are necessary. Without them, the combined effects of the mainsail and jib would tend to bend the top of the mast aft.

Modern boats are usually equipped with lightweight stainless steel stays and shrouds. Stainless steel wire has enormous strength for its weight. It also resists corrosion, and although it does stretch some, this is not usually a critical problem if the stretch is taken into account when tuning the rig.

In general, the beginning sailor is better off keeping

his mast straight. More often than not, this means straight up and down and centered exactly. It is the shrouds that hold the mast straight and in the center of the boat. The mast should not lean or bow either to starboard or port. The drawing shows how the shrouds prevent bowing in the mast. Note that there are two sets of shrouds, upper and lower. The upper shrouds pass over the spreader and support the top of the mast. Under sail, the strain on the upper shroud on the windward side thrusts against the mast through the spreader. This tends to make the mast bow to leeward, To prevent such bowing, the lower windward shrouds are attached to the mast at the base of the spreader. As you can see, the combined effect of the two shrouds is to bold the mast perfectly straight.

One problem every sailor faces is timing his rig; that is, finding the combination of mast rake and tautness of stays and shrouds that gives the best sailing performance, Unfortunately, there are no set rules for tuning. Indeed, there are probably as many theories of tuning as there are sailors. Some prefer the standing rigging to be set up "bar taut," while others insist that slack rigging makes a boat go best.

For the beginning sailor, there is an intermediate choice that will produce good performance with relatively little difficulty. To begin with, the mast must be straight as well as *athwartships* at all times. Obviously, the base of the mast must be securely fastened in its proper position. If it should slip, the entire mast would be out of alignment. The next step is to adjust the shrouds so that the mast stands straight. This is accomplished by means of *turnbuckles,* which are fastened to *chain plates.* On most boats, chain plates are metal straps that run down the side of the hull. They are securely fastened through the hull or deck. You can make certain the mast is centered properly by measuring the distance between the masthead and a similar point on each side of the boat. The two distances, of course, should be equal. The best way to make this measurement is to attach a steel tape measure to the shackle of the main halyard, and then run the shackle up to the masthead.

Finally, it is necessary to adjust the shrouds so that the mast remains straight while under sail. This is the most difficult part of tuning. You will have to take your boat out to check the mast carefully while on several different points of sailing on both tacks. With a reliable crew member at the helm, crawl forward and sight up the mast. If it is bending or leaning to leeward, take up on the windward shrouds until it is straight. If the mast is out of line toward the windward side, loosen the windward shrouds. Once the rig is tuned properly, you will find the leeward shrouds a bit slack, while the windward shrouds are taut. Then, when the boat is on the other tack, the reverse will occur. That is, regardless of whether you are on a starboard or a port tack, the windward shrouds will be taut and the leeward shrouds slightly slack, but the mast will be perfectly straight. In general, the upper shrouds—those leading to the mastbead—should be fairly taut. The lower shrouds should be somewhat less taut than the upper shrouds. This builds in a compensation for stretch in the longer upper shrouds. If the lowers are set up as taut as the uppers, stretch in the uppers will allow the masthead to bend to leeward when the rig is under tension.

Finally, it is necessary to adjust the fore-and-aft position of the masthead. The wisest thing to do here is to follow your boat's sail plan. That is, set the rake of the mast according to the designer's plan. If the design is a good one, this position should produce a satisfactory helm when the boat is going to windward. If it turns out that the boat does not have good balance, that is, that it has excessive weather helm or lee helm, adjustment in the rake of the mast may help.

Both the jibstay and the backstay must be set up quite taut. If your boat has jumper stays, as in the drawing, these should be tightened enough to bend the top of the mast slightly forward before the mast is stepped. The mast will then straighten when the backstay is taken up. There are good reasons for taut stays. If the jibstay is slack, the luff of the jib will sag to leeward. This greatly reduces the jib's efficiency going to windward. If the backstay is slack, on the other hand, the weight of the jib will pull the mast forward, and the set of the mainsail will be disturbed. As you recall, the average mainsail is cut for rise with a straight mast. If the mast should bend or twist, the sail's shape is altered. Wrinkles then occur, as well as hard spots-areas of the sail that are stretched flat, not properly curved. Despite anything that you might read in a book, however, the real test of a tuning job is in the sailing. There is simply no way other than a careful and thorough tuning *under sail* to get the most out of a boat. Many sailors, dissatisfied with their boats, can lay the blame in their own laps for failing to properly tune their rigs.

Running rigging

By removing all of the remaining rigging from the drawing, we have shown just the running rigging. The principal lines in the running rigging are the *halyards,* which pull sails up, and the *sheet lines,* which pull sails in. In addition, there is the *topping lift,* which fields the boom up when the mainsail has been lowered, avid the *outhaul,* which pulls the foot of the mainsail taut along the boom, Finally, *downhauls* pull sails down into positions that produce more effective drive. When a spinnaker is in use, you recall, one of the controlling lines is a *guy line.*

Sheet lines control the position of the sails relative to the wind. Sails may be sheeted in tightly, as when sailing to windward, or sheeted way out, as when running before the wind. There are two problems related to the sheet lines. First, just how much line must be eased out to get the greatest efficiency from the sails? This we will discuss later. Second, where on the boat should the sheet lines lead? Let's consider the jibsheets first.

As the drawing shows, the jibsheets are led to the deck along a line that makes a ten-degree angle from the centerline of the boat. On most boats, the jibsbeet block is fastened to a slide on a track along this line. Thus the problem is one of positioning the slide to get the best performance from the jib.

To find out where the lead should be for your boat, sail the boat as close to the wind as you can, and then very gradually start to *luff up*. If the jibsheet lead is correctly positioned, the jib will luff, that is, begin to flap, along the entire forward edge of the sail. If the jib should luff nearer the foot of the sail first, the lead is too far forward; move the block aft on the track. If the jib should luff nearer the head of the sail first, the lead is too far aft; move the block forward on the track.

There are many different possibilities for rigging the mainsheet. We show three popular arrangements in the drawing. If you look carefully the next time you are in a well-populated harbor, you will see numerous others. How the mainsheet is rigged, however, is less important than how it is used, for the mainsail must be trimmed correctly for maximum efficiency. When sailing to windward, it is important that the full length of the luff of the main enter the wind at the same angle.

Unfortunately, this does not occur perfectly because the upper part of the sail twists away from the wind. But with the head sagging off this way, less sail area is available for generating drive. It's impossible to completely correct this condition., but it can be improved greatly by changing the direction of the pull of the mainsheet in relation to the centerline of the boat.

As the drawing shows, a pull downward on the boom has a flattening effect on the sail. This is what is desired. On the other hand, when the boom is sheeted in on an angle, the end of the boom tends to rise, and the head of the sail sags off. For windward work, then, the rule is trim the boom out-and-down. On many boats the sheet block is attached to a traveler that permits this adjustment. The crew simply slides the block outward away from the centerline of the boat.

When beating in light air, however, a different arrangement is necessary. Under these circumstances, more draft in the sail is required than when sailing closehauled in medium or heavy wind. This additional draft can be produced by moving the mainsheet block in toward the centerline of the boat, thus permitting the boom to lift somewhat. Easing off the clew outhaul a bit helps the situation also. When reaching or running in winds other than very light airs, however, the mainsail should be fairly flat to achieve the best possible performance. Unfortunately, the sheet line is of no help here, for when the boom is trimmed way out, the sheet line pulls in rather than down. Thus some other rig must be used to hold the boom down.

A *boom vang* solves the problem. As the drawing shows, there are a number of different ways to do the job. It's important, however, to be sure the vang rig will go on and come off easily, with little or no chance of tangling. You should also remember that a boom vang puts an enormous strain on the boom, gooseneck fitting, and mast. It should be designed and installed by someone who knows what he is doing.

8

WIND, WATER AND SAIL

Earlier, when we explained how the wind drives a sailboat, we used such terms as *beating, reaching,* and *running.* These terms describe the basic sailing positions relative to the wind. Up to this point it was enough for you to have just a general idea of what they mean. Now it becomes necessary to look more closely at their meanings, for in the next chapter we will be embarking on an imaginary sail. For both this imaginary sail and the real sailing you will do later, a greater knowledge of how the wind and a boat interact is necessary.

The drawing shows the positions of the boat and the sail settings relative to the wind for all courses on the *starboard tack.* When a boat is on the starboard tack, the wind is coming in over the starboard side of the boat. For the *port tack* wind coming in over the port side of the boat—just picture the mirror image of the diagram. All of the positions for the port tack are exactly opposite those shown.

Sailboats are sailed either to *windward or to leeward.* Whenever the bow of the boat is more into the wind than away from the wind, it is sailing to windward. Beating and close reaching are windward courses. The dividing line is the beam reach; when a boat is on a beam reach, the wind is at right angles to the course of the boat. Finally, when the bow of the boat is away from the wind, the boat is sailing to leeward. Broad reaching and running are leeward courses.

Beating

When a boat is beating, it is sailing as close to the wind as possible—but usually not closer than forty-five degrees to the wind direction. Sailing closchauled requires careful attention to several details. As you recall, the main boom is trimmed down-and-out to the lee quarter in order to flatten the mainsail. The jib is sheeted in carefully to produce the best possible slot effect. This is the position of sailing with the greatest sideways effect of the wind's energy; hence it is often necessary to climb up and out on the windward side of the boat to counteract heeling. This is called "hiking out." Several of the pictures in the book show you that hiking out can sometimes be quite an acrobatic stunt.

In order to find the course for beating—that is, to get as close to the wind as possible without luffing—follow these steps. Sheet in the mainsail and jib, and slowly head up into the wind until the mainsail luffs. Then ease off until the luffing stops. This is your course, The sails should be full and drawing well. If you are holding course, but the sail begins to luff, it means the wind has shifted ahead—that is, it has *hauled,* Fall off until the luffing stops, If you suspect that the wind has shifted more toward the stern—that is, *has veered*—head up into the wind until the sail begins to luff. Easing off until the luffing stops then gives you the new course.

When beating, it is important to check the condition of the boat constantly. For example, if you seem to be going too slowly, fall off a bit. It's possible to point too close to the wind; this costs speed. You might also try easing the sheets a bit, because pinching will also slow a boat. Always keep an eye on the forward third of the mainsail. This is where luffing first occurs; it therefore tells you wind direction at once.

Reaching

In general, there are three reaching positions: the *close reach,* the *beam reach,* and the *broad reach.* All lie between beating and running before the wind. In many respects, reaching gives the sailor the most fun for his efforts. The boat usually heels less on a reach than when beating, and goes faster because a greater portion of the total wind force goes into drive. In addition, the boat is usually in better balance on a reach. As a result, handling is easier.

The close reach lies between the beat and the broad reach. To set the sails for a close reach, first put the boat on course. Then ease out the sheets until both the mainsail and jib begin to luff. At this point, haul in the sheets until the fluttering stops. If you have been careful, this should involve hauling in only a few inches of sheet line. On a beam reach the wind is ninety degrees to the course of the boat, or close to it. To set the sails for a beam reach, follow the procedure outlined above for the close reach. On many boats, this is the most exciting point of sailing. It is very fast, and if the rig is tuned properly, quite thrilling.

Your boat is on a broad reach when the wind is coming from aft of the beam but not from directly astern, Once again, the technique in setting the sails is to put the boat on course, ease out the sheets until the sails begin to luff, and then haul in the sheets until the luffing stops. If your boat has a masthead wind pennant, a good rule of thumb is to set the boom at an angle halfway between the line of the keel and the direction the wind pennant is pointing.

In a good breeze, with moderate seas running, a

boat on a broad reach will surf down the front of waves as they pass under the boat. This is indeed exciting sailing,

Running

A sailboat is running before the wind when the wind comes from astern or slightly on the quarter. To set the mainsail, the mainsheet is eased out until the boom is nearly at right angles to the centerline of the boat. If a boom vang is available, this is one time to use it, for the main should be as flat as possible. Without a vang, the boom will ride up and the mainsail will billow. Under these circumstances, the sail will chafe against the shrouds and spreader. This alters the sail's shape and may even result in a tear. The vang also serves to prevent an accidental jibe. The working jib is useless on a run because it is blanketed by the mainsail. It is possible, however, to hold the jib out on the side opposite the main by a pole. The pole—called a *whisker pole*—extends from the clew of the jib to a point somewhere on the mast. A boat sailing this way is said to be sailing *wing-and-wing*.

As picturesque as sailing wing-and-wing is, it is Dot particularly fast, especially in very light winds. Clearly, since the principal driving force when running is the direct pressure of the wind on the sails, to increase speed it is necessary to increase sail area. This is accomplished by flying a spinnaker. The spinnaker markedly increases the speed of a boat when running or broad reaching, for it offers much more sail area to the wind than a working jib. Indeed, you will sometimes see both a spinnaker and a working jib in use, with both sails drawing well.

Wind and a moving boat

Earlier in this chapter we mentioned *hauling* and *veering. The* wind is said to haul when it changes direction toward the bow of the boat. It is said to veer when it changes direction toward the stem. Both of these changes are in relation to the boat. That is, we are looking at wind change from the point of view of the boat.

It is also possible to view change in wind direction from the point of view of the horizon. Suppose the wind is coming from the north—we call this a north wind. Now, when the wind changes in an easterly direction, it is said *to veer. On* the other hand, when it swings to westward, it is said *to back.*

Additional new terminology is needed to describe how the wind comes ill to a moving boat. It may, for example, strike the boat anywhere from dead ahead all the way to dead astern, either on the starboard or port side, The drawing gives these new terms They are exactly the same on the opposite side of the boat.

When the wind is coming from within forty-five degrees of the heading of the boat, it is referred to as *wind ahead.* The forty-five-degree angle may vary. As we have pointed out, most boats will point up to about forty-five degrees to the wind. Some, however, sail closer than forty-five degrees, while many others do not even reach the forty-five-degree mark. When the wind is from the direction at which the boat points most efficiently, the term is on *the wind.*

Between the beating angle and almost directly abeam, the wind is *forward of the beam.* Then, when the wind is directly on the beam—a point ninety degrees from the heading of the boat—it is a *beam* wind. Wind arriving from a direction between ninety and 135 degrees from the bow is wind *abaft the beam. Wind from the quarter is* then wind coming in from 135 to 180 degrees from the heading of the boat. Finally, wind coming from directly behind the boat is called *wind astern.*

Pennants and *telltales*—pieces of cloth ribbon or yarn-attached to the masthead or shrouds indicate the direction of the wind on a boat. It's important to understand, however, that on a moving boat the pennant and telltales do not tell you the true *direction of* the wind. They tell you the direction of the *apparent wind.* Here's why. Look at the drawing. With the true wind on the beam, and the boat sailing forward, the pennant drags behind a bit because it is affected by the air the boat is moving through as well as by the beam wind. The result on the wind pennant is an angle slightly aft of the angle that would have been produced if the boat were standing still. Thus the position of the pennant on a moving boat makes the wind appear to be coming from a point farther ahead than it really is. This is the *apparent wind* direction. Many sailors refer frequently to the telltale while sailing be cause its position is an indication of the direction of the wind relative to the beading of the boat. Thus, as the diagram suggests, the telltale angle can help the skipper bold his course when the wind is constant, and it quickly reveals a wind shift when the wind is variable. A wind shift, of course, should be followed by an adjustment of the sail settings. The beginning sailor in particular will find keeping a close watch on the telltale a good habit to cultivate. In fact, actually sailing a boat in a large circle is a most instructive drill. Try it, and keep a close watch on the behavior of the telltale as the boat changes relative to the wind.

Correcting improper helm

The way the wind interacts with a sailboat produces another important effect. This is the condition of "helm." A boat has helm if it spontaneously turns either into the wind or away from the wind when the tiller is released. If the boat turns into the wind, it is said to have weather *helm.* If it falls off, that is, turns away from the wind, it has lee *helm.* In both instances it is necessary to compensate with the rudder for the turning tendency. But this introduces drag because the rudder is turned while the boat is moving ahead. In the case of extreme helm, the resulting rudder drag can slow the boat down considerably.

A well-balanced boat should have very little helm. Many skippers, however, feel that a small amount of weather helm is desirable, for with it the boat tends to point up to its best position of beating. Lee helm, on the other band, can be downright dangerous. It makes it difficult to bead up into the wind when the boat had been bit by a sudden puff or squall, and could result in a capsize. As you will discover, the first thing to do in a sudden squall is bead up into the wind and ease the sheets. Even more important, should a skipper sailing alone fall overboard, be would have no chance of getting back to a boat with a lee helm, for it would sail away from him.

Let's consider what causes improper helm and then point out bow to correct it. As the drawing shows, a sailboat can be pictured as tending to turn on a vertical axis running down through the boat and center-board. The *center of lateral resistance* of the boat-the point on the hull where a single force would exactly offset all of the side forces on the boat-lies on this axis. Now, if the wind pressure on the sails is exactly the same on either side of the center of lateral resistance, the boat is perfectly balanced; there will be no adverse helm. But if the wind pressure *aft* of the center of lateral resistance is the greater, weather helm results. In effect, the pressure difference drives the boat up into the wind. The reverse condition causes lee helm. The greater wind pressure *forward* of the center of lateral resistance drives the boat away from the wind.

There are several ways to correct adverse helm, Among these are (1) adjusting the jib and mainsail, (2) raising or lowering the center-board, (3) shifting the weight of the crew or movable gear forward or aft, (4) changing the rake of the mast, and (5) moving the jibstay forward or aft. Of these corrective measures, the first three are carried out while under way. If adverse helm can't be satisfactorily corrected by these measures, permanent changes such as the latter two must be carried out.

Let's describe how to correct weather helm first, since this condition i; the one you will most likely have to cope with. Keep in mind that weather helm occurs because there is greater wind pressure on the sails aft of the center of lateral resistance. Easing *the mainsheet* allows wind to spill from the main, thus reducing wind pressure. *Sheeting in the* jib has the effect of increasing wind pressure forward. Either or both of these measures will often greatly improve weather helm. Also try *raising the centerboard* a bit. This shifts the center of lateral resistance aft, but only reduces the area of centerboard in the water a slight amount. Another way to move the center of lateral resistance aft is to *shift the crew or heavy weights aft.* This lowers the stern in the water, and offers more lateral resistance aft than forward.

If these temporary measures fail to correct weather helm to your satisfaction, try the following more permanent adjustments. First, *decrease the rake of the mast,* that is, tip the mast forward a bit by easing up on the backstay and tightening up the jibstay. Don't forget to readjust the shrouds also. A very small change in the rake of the mast shifts a lot of sail area, so carry out this correction with care. On most boats you should not rake the mast forward of the vertical. Finally, you can try *moving the point of attachment of the jibstay forward* at the bow. This shifts sail area forward and reduces weather helm by a leverage effect. It works much the same as increasing the length of a crowbar increases the force that can be applied. In the case of the jib, sail area is moved forward, and greater wind leverage results forward of the center of lateral resistance.

Lee helm, which occurs because wind pressure forward of the center of lateral resistance is greater, is corrected by taking the opposite steps, that is, by moving the center of lateral resistance forward. While under way, try *hauling in the mainsheet* and *slacking the jibsheet. Also lower the centerboard* and *shift crew and movable weights forward.* Don't get the idea that you should do all of these things at once to correct adverse helm. As you come to know your boat, you will acquire a touch for just the right helm. Then, when the helm isn't quite correct, minor adjustment of one of the above controls will bring the helm back to where you want it. The more permanent adjustments for correcting lee helm, of course, are *raking the mast aft* and moving *the jibstay aft.* There are other permanent corrective measures for adverse helm, but they are beyond the scope of this book. If your boat does not respond to the suggestions given here, you should contact the boat's manufacturer for further suggestions.

9

SAILING IN HEAVY WEATHER

Sooner or later every sailor, despite the routine precaution of checking the weather before going out, finds himself sailing in rough weather. Obviously, there are certain dangers associated with sailing under rough conditions. How such experiences turn out depends entirely upon three factors: (1) how well the sailor understands the various wind and sea conditions he can expect to meet, (2) how well he prepares himself, his crew, and his craft for heavy going, and (3) the physical limitations of his sailboat. All three are important. The sturdiest sailboat is useless in a blow if the skipper fails to take measures to make it seaworthy. Let's assume now that we have run into some rough going on our imaginary sail, and discuss what to do about it.

Wind and wave conditions

In general, waves are produced by wind. Over the ocean, strong storm winds build up the long waves commonly referred to as "swell." In addition to these, local winds produce the choppy conditions you are most likely to encounter as a small-boat sailor. The important point to remember is that strong winds produce potentially dangerous waves. Sometimes these conditions come up very suddenly. The alert skipper must be ready to cope with them when they occur.

Both strong winds and the waves they generate pose hazards to the small-boat sailor. Let's look at the types of wind and wave conditions you can expect to meet, and then describe how they can be handled. With respect to wind, you can look for strong, steady winds, or strong, puffy winds. Strong, steady winds occur in large storms, but they also may occur during the clear weather that follows the passage of a cold front. These winds can usually be predicted in advance; thus you should be able to avoid them.

Strong, puffy winds are more hazardous, as well as more difficult to predict. These winds occur in the thunderstorms and in the sudden squalls that sailors run into so often during the passage of weather fronts. It is the changeability of puffy winds that causes difficulty. They vary from extremely strong to light, and change direction rapidly. Thus, if the skipper is not alert, be may be caught in an accidental jibe or be capsized by a sudden puff from a different direction.

On sheltered waters, such as harbors and small lakes, the long waves of the open ocean are not present. In high winds, however, steep, choppy waves often develop. These waves are particularly troublesome because they can come from many different directions. It is very difficult to judge where the next wave will come from; thus the skipper must always be on the lookout,

How do you judge when the wind is too strong for sailing? This depends on the size and sturdiness of your boat, plus your ability as a sailor. A reliable indicator, however, is the presence of whitecaps. The beginner in a small boat should consider staying in port or coming in at once if the water is covered with whitecaps.

For more experienced sailors, it is possible to sail under more strenuous conditions. In fact, some of the most exciting sailing is done in good, stiff breezes. When the wind is blowing at eleven to sixteen knots, whitecaps first appear. This is a "moderate breeze" on the Beaufort Wind Scale. For boats under twelve feet in length, sailing is potentially hazardous in a moderate breeze,

In a "fresh breeze" the length of the waves has increased, and whitecaps cover the water. Gusts, however, are often considerably stronger than twenty-one knots, Sailing under these conditions is usually safe for skillful sailors in boats sixteen to twenty feet in length, but the going is rough and wet. Small boats should not be out in winds in excess of twenty-one knots, for the danger may be too great.

Beefing

The wind is up, and the going is rough. We elect to adjust by reducing the sail area exposed to the wind. With shortened sails, sailing in high winds is considerably safer because both speed and angle of heel decrease. The boat is thus a lot easier to handle. There are two ways to shorten sail. One of these is to use sails with a smaller surface area. In addition, many skippers carry smaller mainsails for use in windy weather. The second way to reduce sail area is *reefing*, 'l'his is simply a technique for furling or rolling tip a portion of the sail in use.

Many newer boats have *roller reefing* for both the mainsail and jib. For the mainsail, the boom is specially rigged at the gooseneck and the sheet attachment so that it can be rolled like a window shade. To reef the main, the sail is luffed and then lowered gradually while the crew rolls it up on the boom. As this is being done, the sail must be pulled out toward the clew to smooth out wrinkles and prevent folding or bunching. A mainsail rigged for roller reefing is quite convenient, for it eliminates the need to change sails. Roller reefing is also easier than tying in reef points, the older method for reefing the main.

More and more boats today are being equipped with roller reefing jibs. These rigs solve two problems. They permit the skipper to shorten sail on the jib without leaving the cockpit, and they provide a neat and simple way to furl and store the jib. In operation, the roller reefing jib winds up on the jibstay when the sail is shortened. The jib is then unfurled by drawing on the sheet line after releasing the furling line.

In the older, more conventional method of reefing the mainsail, one or more lines of reef points are sewn into the sail parallel to the boom Reef points are small cords sewn into patches set into the sail. Large brass rings, called *cringles,* are set into the sail at either end of the line of reef points. The forward cringle is the luff *cringle,* the after one is the *leech cringle.*

Not all sailboats have reef points in their sails. Enough do, however, to make a description of their use worthwhile. Try to remember that if it is necessary to reef, it is a lot easier to do it before going out. Reefing while out in rough weather can be a difficult and potentially hazardous task.

The steps in reefing the main are as follows. Since we are already out on the water, first luff the main. Next, lower the mainsail partially, and draw the sail up to the boom along the line of reef points. Lash the luff cringle to the boom as shown in the drawing, and follow by lashing the leech cringle to the outhaul and around the boom. Now pull out and flatten the fold of sail formed by tying down the cringles.

Furl the folded-off portion of the sail into a tight

cylinder. With the furled sail in place, start at the luff and tie reef points around it, Use a square knot and tie the reef points around the sail only, *not* around the boom. If your sail is equipped with grommets without reef points, start at the forward end of the sail and pass a lacing around the furled sail, but not around the boom. Tie the lacing at the clew.

Avoid leaving a reef in a sail any longer than is necessary, for it can distort the shape of the sail. Shaking out a reef is quite simple. Just reverse the steps in tying in the reef. Untie the reef points, release the outhaul and luff lashings, and then raise the sail all the way. Take care to be sure all lashings and reef points have been released before raising the sail.

Heavy weather sailing tactics

In addition to reefing, several sailing tactics will help us stay under control in the strong winds we have encountered. Before discussing these tactics, however, we want to emphasize again what to do when your boat is hit by a sudden and very strong puff of wind. First, *head up into the wind* to take the puff head on. Second, *release the sheet lines* to spill the wind out of the sails. In practice, you will learn to release the sheets just as the boat acquires enough momentum to carry the bow up into the wind.

If the wind should become too strong for reefing sails or jib alone, we can drop the mainsail first and then the jib, and then run before the wind under bare poles. If speed becomes excessive, the boat may broach or take heavy seas from astern. To slow the boat down trail a long line, a bucket, or a sea anchor over the stern.

If it is necessary to go to windward with full sail in strong winds, try sailing on a tight jib and a luffing mainsail, This tactic is called the "fisherman's reef." With the main eased out and luffing, the sail's drive is sharply reduced. At the same time, however, it still has some drive in the leech. In addition, the jib will backwind the main, also cutting down on the drive of the sails. With less drive, the boat will sail in a more erect position, and also sail slower. In heavy weather it is necessary to reduce speed to minimize slamming into head seas. While sailing under a fisherman's reef, remember to bold the main and jibsheets by band, with only a turn of the line around a cleat or winch. You must be ready to release the sheets at once if the wind becomes too strong.

The safest point of sailing in strong winds is *broad reaching.* This is true partly because the boat is erect when broad reaching, and partly because the skipper can play the sails against the wind. In strong puffs, the sheets are eased out and the boat is luffed up. On the other hand, when the wind softens, the sheets are hauled and the boat may be returned to its course. Both the main and the jib should be eased out until they luff, with just the after portions of the sails supplying drive. Sailed this way, broad reaching under rough going allows a maximum of' control over varying wind conditions.

If the wind is too strong for reefing or one of the other tactics for sailing under full sail, it is possible to sail under either the mainsail or the jib alone. If your desired course will permit you to sail on a reach, you will have more control of the boat under main alone than under jib alone. You can play the varying strength of the wind as in broad reaching, In addition, because the sail area is concentrated aft of the center of lateral resistance, the boat will have a strong weather helm, and thus head up into the wind quite easily.

If it is possible for you to run before the wind,

sailing under the jib alone is relatively safe in strong winds. If your boat is not equipped with a storm jib; the working jib alone provides the smallest possible amount of sail area. Running or broad reaching under jib alone is steady and fairly easy to manage. It is much more difficult to control the course of the boat when beam reaching or going to windward on jib alone, for the boat will make more leeway than usual. In addition, the helmsman will be working with a lee helm, which, as we have pointed out, is undesirable.

If the wind becomes so strong that running with jib alone or under bare poles is dangerous, that is, if the boat threatens to turn broadside to the waves and be swamped, it will be necessary to trail some sort of sea *anchor* over the stern. This will slow the boat down and will probably bold the stern to the waves. Various types of sea anchors are available. One is shown in the drawing. The speed of a boat running with a sea anchor out is controlled by the trip line of the anchor. By pulling on the trip line, the anchor is spilled and the boat moves faster. As mentioned earlier, dragging anything over the stern, from a long line to a swamped dinghy, serves as a sea anchor. Let's hope that you are never in the unfortunate position of requiring a sea anchor. In general, careful attention to the weather *before going* out can prevent such mishaps.

What to do when capsized

The commonest reaction to a capsize, especially from beginners, is surprise. They all say they bad no idea it was about to happen. Center-board boats capsize for a variety of reasons. A sudden puff of wind too strong for the sail area carried, too little speed, failure to rebalance crew weight while coming about, and jibing in a strong wind with the centerboard tip are just a few. In the case of beginning sailors, inexperience and misjudgment of wind and sea conditions are also important factors.

We can't emphasize too strongly the importance of preventing a capsize. The box summarizes what you should do to minimize the chances of capsizing. Read its contents carefully. In a nautical paraphrase of Smokey the Bear, "Only you can prevent a capsize." Unfortunately, capsizing can be as great a disaster as a forest fire in terms of loss of life. Very few people seem to know the correct things to do after they have been dumped into the water.

The most important rule is *"Stay with the Boat."* Obviously, this refers to a boat that will support the entire crew when it is swamped. A recent tragedy on Lake Michigan illustrates just bow important this rule is. Two boys and a girl capsized in a small sailboat within view of about twenty people on shore. A rescue operation was started at once, but the only boat available bad a balky engine that would not start. In the fifteen minutes it took to start the engine, both boys had drowned. They had started swimming for shore thinking that it was only a couple of hundred yards away. Both boys were excellent swimmers, but that "couple of hundred yards" turned out to be something over a mile. When the girl was finally picked up, she reported that one of the boys bad called the other "chicken" because he had wanted to stay with the boat rather than strike out for shore.

Again and again lives are lost because people leave capsized boats. They don't realize that most boats will float even when swamped, and that it is far safer to stay with a swamped boat than to attempt to swim to shore. In the case of sailboats, it is often possible to right the boat and then sit on the floor of the cockpit. To right a boat, the first step is to get the sails down. The centerboard is then forced down all the way, thus providing a point of leverage for righting the hull. As the drawing shows, the crew should stand on the centerboard and apply downward pressure while *holding* on at the coaming. With the boat righted, the entire crew can usually sit inside the cockpit without sinking the boat.

In the unlikely event that a swamped sailboat isn't rescued right away, it may even be possible to bail it out. Stuff clothing, sail bags, or even sail into the top of the centerboard well, and hang onto the outside of the boat. If the waves are not too high, you may be able to splash and bail water from the cockpit fast enough to stay ahead of incoming water. Bailing out a swamped boat is time-consuming and exhausting work, however, and should only be tried as a last resort. It is much better to save your strength and wait for rescue.

10 PREPARING FOR A SAIL

At last we are ready to get out on the water—in an imaginary way, of course. Many things, however, most be done before sailing away from a mooring or dock in a safe and seaworthy manner, It is important that you learn to perform all of these steps faithfully. Overlooking one or more may ruin your sailing fun by leading to a mishap of some sort. We will point out potential accidents as we go along.

To begin with, we assume that the boat is properly equipped with all of the required Coast Guard approved safety equipment, especially life jackets. In addition, there should be at least one paddle and a bucket or bilge pump aboard, plus an anchor and sufficient anchor line for the depth of water to be sailed on. If your boat is large enough, an outboard engine may be desirable. We can't emphasize too strongly the need for adequate safety equipment. Altogether too many boating accidents occur because the minimum required safety equipment was not on board.

To begin our first sail, we have to get out to the boat. This is no problem if it is tied up to a dock or in a slip, but may be one if it is necessary to row a dinghy out to a mooring. Don't overload the dinghy. An overloaded dinghy has very little freeboard, and is very unstable. Many a picnic lunch and many a bundle of dry gear, plus two or three unhappy sailors, have wound up in the drink because a dinghy was overloaded. Make two trips or more if necessary.

Having gotten aboard the boat safely, several chores must be performed before bending on the sails. First, of course, the cockpit cover must be removed and stowed away. All loose gear on a sailboat should be carefully stowed away. The gear and rigging essential to sailing take up enough room without additional clutter. Next, lower the centerboard or daggerboard. This adds stability to the boat and prevents it from tipping too much as you move about. Now check the bilge for water. There may be either seepage or some accumulated rainwater. Pump out or sponge up any water; one mark of a good sailor is a dry boat. Finally, attach the tiller and rudder if this is necessary. On many smaller boats it is customary to store the tiller and rudder on the cockpit floorboards. Be careful when you climb aboard, Stepping down hard on a rudder or tiller can produce serious damage.

Bending on the mainsail

When a sloop is on a mooring and pointing into the wind, the rule is to raise the mainsail first. The general rule, in fact, is to raise the sails in a direction against the wind. Thus, when the bow points into the wind, the sails are raised going forward, the main first, the jib last. If the jib is raised first, the wind may cause the boat to turn and sail downwind. On the other hand, if the boat is pointed downwind, the jib is raised first. When we discuss leaving the mooring or dock the reasons for these rules will become clearer.

The sequence of steps for bending on and raising the mainsail are, as follows. First, set the main in its sailbag beneath the *gooseneck fitting*—that is, beneath the point where the mast and boom come together. Unfasten the main halyard, make sure it is free aloft, and then attach it to the headboard of the sail. Do not, however, raise the sail at this point. Now draw the sail out of the bag, running your hand along the luff to make sure there are no, snags or twists. Straighten out any twists before attempting to run the sail slides onto the track on the mast. After running all the slides on the track in the proper order, close the *slide stop* at the bottom of the track. This will keep the slides on the track and the sail in position along the luff for raising.

The next step is bending the foot of the sail on the boom. Begin by fastening the tack of the sail to the gooseneck fitting. Now run the entire foot of the sail through your hands to make sure it is straight and that no slides are twisted. Starting with the slide closest to the clew of the sail, thread the slides along the foot out onto the boom. The boom crutch should remain in place while this is being done. Now fasten the clew to the *outhaul fitting. Pull* the outhaul hand tight and cleat it. At this point, slide the battens into their sleeves along the leech of the sail, making sure that they are correctly fastened in place.

It's a good idea to mark the head, tack, and clew on your sails with indelible ink. Simply print the letters H, T, and C on the sailcloth near the corners of the sail. This will make it much easier for you to bend on sail directly from the sailbag. Do this for all of your sails, on both sides, but code the spinnaker on one side only. If you don't, you may find one of its corners twisted when you set the sail. Also, do not label the lower spinnaker corners T and C; P and S for port and starboard are better.

If your boat has a slotted mast and boom, there will be no sail slides. Instead, the bolt rope along the foot and luff of the sail is threaded into the slot, with the foot going on first. The one difference in the procedure is that you do not attach the luff of the sail to the mast before raising the sail. The bolt rope is threaded into the slot on the mast as the sail is raised. The simplest procedure is to have your crew feed the sail into the slot as you hoist the sail aloft. The next step is raising the sail. Leave the boom crutch in position while the sail is being raised to prevent it from being stretched, but: clear and slack the mainsheet. The sheet line Should run through the proper fittings and be clear of the tiller and centerboard well. Tie a figure-eight knot in the end of the mainsbeet to prevent it from running through the blocks. To put enough slack into the sheet, lift the boom overhead, and then replace it in the boom crutch. The last preparatory step to raising the main is releasing the downhaul. This will be tightened down to stretch the luff after the sail has been raised as far as it will go.

Hoist the sail, watching it carefully as you do. Make sure the slides are not twisted and that the battens are free of the spreader and shrouds as the sail goes up. The last one or two inches may be difficult, requiring a strong effort on your part. With the sail set up, lift the boom out of the crutch, stow the crutch in the cockpit, and allow the boom to fly. Watch out for your head!! Secure the halyard to its cleat, coil the line, and stow it in the bottom of the boat. Be sure to coil and stow the halyard so that it can be released instantly. The last step is adjusting the downhaul. Take up on the downhaul until the luff of the sail begins to wrinkle.

Bending on the jib

With the mainsail in position and properly adjusted, bend on and raise the jib. As the drawing shows, the sequence of the steps is as follows. First, place the jib in its bag on the foredeck, with the open end of the bag facing forward. Pull out the jib tack and shackle it to the deck fitting. Now draw the luff of the jib out of the bag and fasten the jib hooks to the jibstay. Start at the tack of the sail and work up, fastening the hooks in order. Make sure that the hooks all go on in the same direction and that the sail is not twisted, Free the jib halyard, make sure it is clear aloft, and fasten it to the head of the sail.

If your jib has battens, now is the time to put them in place. In any event, remove the remainder of the jib from the bag, stow the bag, and fasten the jibsheets to the clew of the sail. The sheet lines should be slack. Be sure the sheets are rigged correctly. On some boats they go outside the shrouds, on others inside the shrouds. Now raise the jib, keeping an eye on the sail as you do to make sure everything is in proper order. Take up the jib halyard so that the luff wire of the sail is taut, If the luff of the sail is loose and "scalloped," it will be far less efficient than when it is set up properly.

Be careful when you are handling halyards. On some boats, if you let the shackle go, the weight of the halyard will pull it up the mast. It may then jam in the sheave at the top of the mast. When this happens, it is almost impossible to shake the shackle loose. On small boats, you can beach the craft and tip it on its side to retrieve the halyard shackle. On larger boats, someone usually has to go up the mast, although it is occasionally possible to heel the boat close enough to a roof or bridge to recover the shackle. The best procedure is to be alert to the possibility of losing the shackle, and thus make sure it does not happen. Well, there you are, the centerboard is down, the rudder and tiller are attached, and the sails have been hoisted. You're ready to cast off and sail away. Or are you? A moment's thought should tell you that although the boat may be ready to go, the skipper shouldn't be—not without a final check. First, check everything you did while making ready. Are the sails set properly? Is all the loose gear stowed away? Are the life jackets or Coast Guard approved safety cushions within easy reach? Is the paddle on board for use should the wind fail? Is the engine in operating condition? Is the rudder and tiller assembly functioning correctly? Are the sheet lines free and ready to use? Next, check the weather. Has the wind come up? Is a thunderstorm on its way toward you? You would be surprised at the number of sailors who cast off in the face of a storm because they were so engrossed with raising the sails that they failed to check the weather.

Leaving the mooring

We will consider two situations at a mooring: (1) the boat is pointing *into the wind* at the mooring, regardless of the strength and direction of the water current, and (2) the boat is pointing *downwind* at the mooring because the wind and current are opposite to each other, with the current stronger than the wind. Let's look at the first instance; it is the situation you will most frequently find yourself in.

You are ready to drop the mooring when the skipper is at the tiller and controls the mainsbeet, and the crew is forward ready to release the mooring buoy. The first step is to cast off and drift straight back to clear the mooring. Next, put the *jib aback* to turn the bow of the boat in the desired direction. With the bow turned, haul on the sheets to adjust the sails for a reach. Sail this way until the boat has picked up enough speed to adjust the sails for the desired course. Oh yes, you should have figured out where you wanted to go before leaving the mooring.

Let's take a closer look at the technique of putting

the jib aback. This is a very easy maneuver for turning the bow of a boat when it is pointing into the wind. Make sure the jibsheets are loose and not cleated. Now grasp the clew of the jib and hold it out to the side opposite the direction the bow is to turn. If the boat has sternway, it will help to put the tiller over in the direction the bow is to swing. The wind will fill the jib and force the bow over. Just as soon as the boat has swung around to the point where a course can be sailed, let go the clew of the jib, put the tiller amidships, and haul the mainsheet and jibsheet so that the sails will fill and the boat will hold the desired course.

An altogether different technique is required to leave a mooring when the boat is pointing downwind. In this case the stern is pointing into the wind; thus the jib is raised first. Allow the jib to fly forward. Bend the mainsail to the mast and boom, but do not raise it while the boat is on the mooring. Leave the boom in its boom crutch. It is very difficult to hoist a mainsail downwind. In addition, once it fills with wind, it will drive the boat around wildly on the mooring. With the jib raised, drop the mooring buoy and haul the jibsheet until the sail fills. This will put you on a downwind tack under the jib alone. Sail on this tack until you are free of other boats and then round up into the wind. At this point, raise the mainsail as quickly as you can. Allow enough room, for the boat will drift some during the maneuver. Next, put the jib aback to turn the bow to your desired course, haul the sheets to a reaching position, and sail away. Finally, readjust the sails to the desired course once you have enough steerage way.

Both leaving a dock and landing at a dock under sail are more difficult than the same maneuvers at a mooring. This is particularly true of landing at a dock, for it is difficult to judge a boat's momentum. Thus, very often a boat will either fetch up short of the dock or ram it with a resounding thump. At this point, however, we are still concerned with getting under way on our imaginary sail.

As the drawing shows, we will describe techniques for casting off a dock under four different wind conditions: (1) wind directly on the dock (a lee dock), (2) wind directly off the dock, (3) wind ahead of the boat, and (4) wind astern of the boat. One of these techniques will handle any wind direction other than those discussed. You will have to determine the one to use as you evaluate the wind. While we discuss what to do under each of these wind conditions, remember that you should try whenever possible to land at a dock with the boat headed into the wind. This makes getting away much easier.

Getting away from a lee dock may present a problem because the wind tends to hold the boat against the dock. If the wind is light enough, you may be able to paddle clear and then head up into the wind to raise the sails. It is also sometimes possible to sail away from a lee dock on the main alone, Have your crew push the bow away as you haul on the mainsheet. If the wind is not too strong, this should enable you to sail the boat clear before using the jib. If the wind is strong, you will have to *kedge out* from the dock before raising the sails. Using a dinghy, carry the anchor out fifty or seventy feet from the dock, and drop the anchor overboard. Your crew then hauls on the anchor line to pull the boat away from the dock. Once clear of the dock and other obstructions, raise sails and up anchor, then sail away just as you would leave a mooring.

Casting off is quite simple when the wind is directly off a dock. Raise the jib only, and cast off the bowline first. Hauling the jibsheet will allow the sail to fill and swing the bow out, With the boat pointing downwind, cast off the stern line and sail downwind on the jib alone. Once the boat is clear of all obstacles, round up into the wind to raise the main. From this point on, the technique is the same as leaving a mooring downwind. The most desirable wind condition for getting away from a dock is wind dead ahead of the boat, Both main and jib can be raised; the boat can then be sailed clear by putting the jib aback, pushing the bow out with a boathook, and hauling sheets to leave the dock on a reach. It will help to use a stern line or spring *line* to hold the stem in place while the bow swings out. Be sure the line is fastened to the cleat or pile so that it can be released instantly from the boat.

Another difficult situation is wind dead astern, or nearly so. As in the case of wind directly off the dock, it will be necessary in this instance to sail away from the dock on the jib alone. The main is not to be raised until the boat has been sailed clear and up into the wind. Again using a stern line or spring line, push the bow away from the dock using a boathook, and haul on the jibsheet until the jib fills and begins to draw the boat away from the dock. Drop the stern line, and sail free on the jib alone. Once you are clear of other obstructions, head up into the wind and raise the main.

Well, it took a bit of doing, but we are finally "under way." The weather is fine, the wind is just right, the sails are set properly, and all safety gear is aboard and within reach. We are free to sail where we please. But as you will see, there is a bit more to it than Just pointing the boat in the direction we want to sail. In the next chapter we tackle the problem of "getting there from here" in a sailboat.

11

READING THE WEATHER

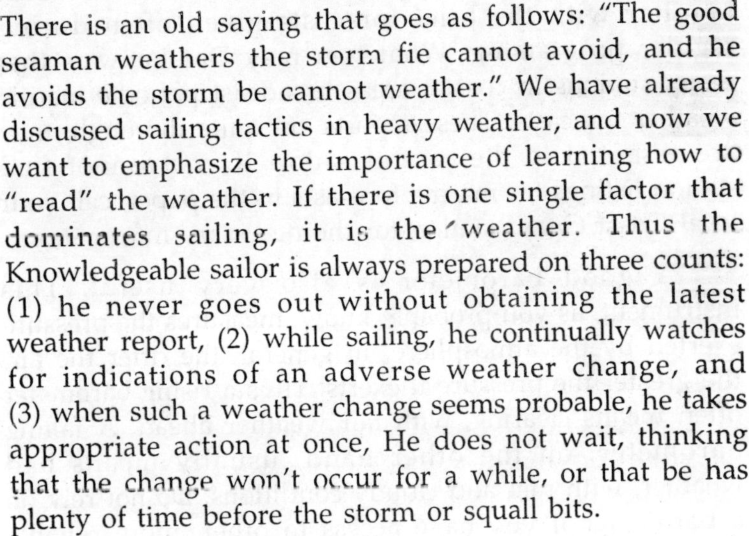

There is an old saying that goes as follows: "The good seaman weathers the storm fie cannot avoid, and he avoids the storm be cannot weather." We have already discussed sailing tactics in heavy weather, and now we want to emphasize the importance of learning how to "read" the weather. If there is one single factor that dominates sailing, it is the ´weather. Thus the Knowledgeable sailor is always prepared on three counts: (1) he never goes out without obtaining the latest weather report, (2) while sailing, he continually watches for indications of an adverse weather change, and (3) when such a weather change seems probable, he takes appropriate action at once, He does not wait, thinking that the change won't occur for a while, or that be has plenty of time before the storm or squall bits.

Keeping on top of the weather is by no means as difficult as it may seem. This is particularly true of obtaining weather reports before going out, for a number of sources are readily available. Virtually every newspaper contains a daily weather map that gives the weather situation throughout the entire country. What is just as important, however, is that these maps allow rough weather predictions for up to a day or so in advance. Become familiar with the map in your local paper. Learn the symbols, and study the map daily for a period of weeks or months. This will establish in your mind the normal weather patterns for your area, and enable you to make a reasonably good prediction on any given day. Television weather reports and forecasts are perhaps even better, for they provide a more up-to-date analysis of the local situation. Many of these programs, as you know, include a thorough weather-map analysis. If you plan to go sailing the following day, Make it a practice to watch the TV weather report the night before.

Radio forecasts are also important. You are no doubt familiar with the brief forecasts given often during regular programing. What you may Dot know is that many stations in coastal areas broadcast periodic marine weather forecasts. These reports are quite thorough; they are essential to the careful sailor. If you cannot find station listings for marine forecasts in the paper, call your local Coast Guard station for the necessary information.

A good barometer is also very useful. This instrument, as you probably know, measures the pressure exerted by the atmosphere. In general, the drier the air, the greater the pressure it exerts. Thus a rising barometer often means clearing, with fair weather ahead. A falling barometer, on the other hand, usually means bad weather, with rain and cloudy conditions. Do not rely on a barometer if you have access to other, more reliable sources of weather information. A barometer allows a very rough forecast only; it should not be looked upon as an infallible instrument.

As you will see later in this chapter, clouds are also good indicators of what the weather holds. There are many different types of clouds, although just three types are enough to provide visible evidence of what is taking place, and what is to take place shortly. Cloud changes, in particular, are useful for signaling weather changes while you are out on the water, In fact, if you have been out sailing for many hours, and you do not have a radio on board, the clouds are probably the only indication you have of an impending weather change. We will see just how shortly.

Weather partners

Weather systems in the United States move from west to east, This general movement is caused by the westerlies prevailing winds that result from the earth's rotation. In addition, the heating effect of the sun and the interaction of high and low-pressure areas produce weather changes.

As you may know, the weather we experience is the result of alternating high and low-pressure areas passing overhead. That is, "lows" are usually followed by "highs." When the pressure is high, the weather is generally good. On the other hand, the weather is usually poor when a low is centered overhead.

Highs and lows are characterized by a particular type of air movement. As the drawing shows, the wind blows in a clockwise direction around a high, but also toward the outside. This is called *anticyclonic rotation.* The wind around a low, on the other hand, blows in a counterclockwise direction in toward the low-pressure center. This movement is called *cyclonic rotation.* A hurricane is simply a cyclonic storm of great intensity. As the warm, moist air rotates toward the center of any low system, the air begins to rise. But in rising it is cooled. Then, when sufficient cooling has occurred, moisture condenses and clouds and rain result.

A closer look at the diagram will suggest one or two additional clues to the weather. For example, along the East Coast strong northeast winds usually mean increasing cloudiness and rain. In New England such storm systems are referred to as "nor'easters." When the wind then shifts to northwest, it usually means the passage of a low and the approach of a high. Clearing generally follows, and fair weather can be expected until the next low arrives.

So far we have described the air mass movements that produce weather changes over very wide areas. The wind of a nor'easter and the brisk northwest breeze that follows passage of a cold front are results of these major air movements, On a smaller scale, the sailor can also look for two ty] · ·s of local breezes, both of which can affect his sailing pleasure. These two breezes are called the *land breeze* and the *sea breeze.*

Land and sea breezes occur near the coastline. Indeed, the story is that fore-and-aft rigs were originally developed in this country to take advantage of the land and sea breezes along our seacoasts and on the Great Lakes. These breezes develop because water and land differ in their capacity to absorb and hold beat. Water absorbs beat from the sun much more slowly than land, but it also holds the beat much longer. Let's start our description at a point in time when the water and land temperatures are about the same-an hour or so before midnight.

As the night hours pass, the land continues to cool. The water just offshore, however, does not lose heat as fast. The result is that around midnight the air above the water is wanner than the air above the adjacent land area. But warm air rises. Thus the air above the water rises, and the cooler air over the land area moves in beneath it. This cool air in motion off the land is the land breeze. Of course, as the cool air comes in contact with the warmer water, it is also warmed. It then rises, and the cycle continues.

After sunrise, the land warms up rapidly. On a bright, sunny day it is usually warmer than the adjacent water sometime around noon. At this point a sea breeze begins. The warm air over the land rises, and cooler air moves off the water to take its place. Anyone who has been to the beach on a bright, warm day is familiar with sea breezes. They usually blow briskly through the afternoon, and then die down around sundown. The greater the temperature difference between land and water, the stronger the breeze.

Many sailors have learned to depend upon afternoon sea breezes to get them home. On Long Island Sound, for example, the afternoon sea breeze from the south is practically a tradition. Local sailors call it the "homing" breeze; they are greatly disappointed if it does not appear "on time" to get them into port before dusk.

Fronts

With major air masses rotating around highs and lows, contact between two masses of air with differing temperatures is inevitable, Such a collision is called a *front.* There are four types of front-cold, warm, *occluded,* and *stationary.*

As far as the sailor is concerned, the cold front is the most important, for it is usually accompanied by violent thunderstorms. A cold front is produced when a cold air mass meets and thrusts under a warm air mass. Because the colder air is heavier, it stays close to the ground, but forces the warm, moist air rapidly to high altitudes. As the warm air rises and cools, its moisture condenses, forming thunder-head clouds. Severe thunderstorms often result.

A warm front results when warm air rides up and over a mass of cold air. The warm air, usually laden with moisture, then cools, and the moisture condenses. Cloudiness and rain are the result, Sometimes a fast-moving cold front will overtake a warm front moving in the same direction. When this happens, the cold air in front and behind the warm air forces the warm air upward. This is called an occluded front. Such fronts may behave as cold fronts or warm fronts or both. Finally, when a cold front and a warm front meet head on and interlock, the result is a stationary front. It helps to know the type of weather frontal conditions will bring. In particular, you should be wary of any approaching cold front, for the thunderstorms it brings are often very severe and dangerous.

Clouds and storms

Of the many different cloud types, three are of particular importance to the sailor. These are the cumulonimbus, or thunderhead; the cumulus; and the cirrus clouds. Cumulonimbus clouds are the massive vertical thunderhead clouds associated with the violent thunderstorms mentioned earlier. All sailors must learn to recognize these clouds, for the storms they bring can be very dangerous to a boat under sail.

The typical thunderstorm occurs during the summer months, usually late in the day. These storms make their first appearance as a darkening sky, usually in the northwest. Often, however, the first warning of an approaching thunderstorm may be AM radio static. Static may develop up to ten hours prior to the storm itself. Following the darkening sky, the typical anvil-shaped, towering thunderhead appears. The cloud is dark and "dirty" along its bottom, with violent wind gusts, heavy rain, and whitecaps underneath. The top is anvil-shaped, but sometimes the cloud is so tall this formation isn't visible. Very often these storms advance in a sharply defined front-an awesome sight to anyone who has witnessed it at sea.

When the storm hits, usually no more than a half hour after one sights the thunderhead, there will be violent winds from several different directions and usually drenching rain. In one thunderstorm we rode out at anchor, the rain was so heavy it was impossible to see the stern of the boat from the cabin—a distance of some seven feet! Waves are generally not a problem, for these storms come up too quickly to generate much wave action.

The winds in thunderstorms are so violent and erratic it is very important to prepare properly for the arrival of the storm. *Under no circumstances should you attempt to sail through a thunderstorm.* If you are close enough to shore—be it a sandy beach, a sheltered cove, or home port—get in as quickly as possible, and get the sails down. If there isn't time to reach shore or home port, drop the sails and lash them down securely. Then anchor and stay put until the storm has passed over.

If the thunderstorms you are caught in are the result of isolated masses of hot air rising into colder air, you can expect them to pass over quickly. These are the typical late afternoon storms of a hot summer day. Storms associated with a cold front, however, may take longer to clear out. As you may know, these storms are spread out along the entire cold front. They are more violent than the local thunderstorm, but they can be avoided, for an advancing cold front is usually forecast well in advance.

Cumulus clouds are fair weather clouds, These are the bright, "cottony" clouds seen on fair, sunny days. They have softly rounded edges, but near the horizon they are flat along the bottom, As long as cumulus clouds are in the sky, there is little chance of any change in the weather. It pays to keep an eye on cumulus clouds, however. Sometimes one can grow tall enough to reach elevations where the temperature is below freezing. When this happens, the innocent fair weather cumulus cloud can develop into the dangerous cumulonimbus thunderhead cloud.

Cirrus clouds generally indicate a change in weather, usually for the worse. These clouds are thin and wispy. A sky with cirrus clouds is often called a "mare's tail" sky, because of its similarity to the feathery wisps of a streaming horse's tail. Cirrus clouds occur at altitudes of twenty thousand to twenty-five thousand feet. They often indicate cloudy, rainy weather within a day or so,

Storm warnings

Always check the weather report before going out sailing. In addition, check for storm warnings at a nearby yacht club or marina. Administered by the U. S. Weather Bureau, storm warning stations are located along the East and West Coasts, on the Great Lakes, and in Hawaii and Puerto Rico. The warnings consist of flags or pennants for the daytime and lights for nighttime. As the illustration shows, there are four warnings—small craft, gale, storm, and *hurricane.* You should commit these signals to memory, and never forget to check before going out sailing.

The most important warning for the small-boat sailor is the small craft warning. This signal, when posted, covers a wide range of wind and/or sea conditions. In addition, the term "small craft" includes boats of many different sizes and types. To be on the safe side, always get a detailed weather forecast before going out when the small craft warning pennant is flying. Wind and sea conditions may or may not be too severe for your boat—you won't be able to tell from the warning signal alone. You will have to match experience with a detailed weather report to estimate the danger correctly. For example, on a given day wind and sea conditions might be very hazardous for a twenty-foot

centerboard boat, but merely exciting and stimulating for a twenty-foot keel boat.

Tide and current

A brief word about the tides and the water movements they cause is in order at this point. Strictly speaking, *tide is* the vertical rise and fall of a body of water, Tide is caused by the gravitational pull of the moon, and to a lesser extent that of the sun, on a body of water. When the sun and the moon are in line with the earth, their combined pull is greater. Hence, the tidal range is greater. Such tides are called spring *tides.* On the other band, when the sun, moon, and earth form a right angle in space—that is, when they are not in a line—the tidal range is smallest. These tides are called *neap tides.*

Current is the horizontal flow of water. When the tide changes at high tide, and the water begins to drop, it can only drop by flowing horizontally out of or away from the bay or inlet it had flooded. Current caused by tidal changes is called *tidal current,* The current of a river or stream is not associated in any way with the tide; it is caused by gravitational force only. Of course, many rivers that empty into the ocean experience tides. On the Connecticut River, for example, the effect of the tide is quite noticeable as far north as Hartford, a distance of some forty miles from the mouth of the river.

12

ENJOYING SAILING

Sailing has always held an attraction for many people. Many dream of some day sailing around the world. Few people do it, but a lot of people enjoy the quiet tranquillity of a summer evening, sifting along in a gentle breeze at sunset, hearing only the gentle lap of the bow wave. Some people enjoy the challenge of the wind and waves, and others like to develop their technical skills to turn the invisible power of the wind into exciting sport and recreation.

The excitement of a long line of boats approaching the starting line, each looking for the ideal start at full speed in clean air, is something you must experience to appreciate. For some, it becomes like an obsession to either race or to be in a boat away from the rest of the everyday world. We can enjoy it more if we can avoid most of the fears, dangers, frustrations, fatigue and personal hang ups. This chapter deals with things that make it more enjoyable, once we know how to avoid the problems. There are so many different ways to enjoy sailing, but you have to choose a suitable boat for your needs, get the boat to the water, plan cruises, get in shape for the physical activity and get along with your crew. Perhaps some of the ideas given will make it easier.

Choosing a boat

There are many questions to consider before deciding on

what boat to buy. You should first try to narrow it down to a decision between a keelboat or a centreboard boat.

(1) *Advantages of a Centreboard Boat:*
Lower cost between $1,200 and $5,000 new, a fraction of the cost of a keelboat and lower mooring, maintenance and equipment costs.

Can be combined with summer cottage life for water recreation or racing. The boat can be dry sailed, so that constant mooring supervision is not necessary at a distance.

Can be a one-man boat to eliminate problems of finding a crew.

Can suit the needs of a family of four for a few hours of day sailing without much preparation of food and equipment.

Can be easily maintained if of fiberglass construction. If plywood, it can be maintained at home.

Can be transported by trailer each time you sail or go to camp or to holiday sites.

Can be a fast racing boat, easily capsized and easily righted, or a more stable boat, broader and with less sail area.

Can be used for cruising with proper care and preparation. Wayfarer class has many cruising enthusiasts.

Risk of fire, explosion, going aground is very small.

Many opportunities for inexpensive racing are available.

(2) *Advantages of a Keelboat*
Can be kept near home at a yacht club or marina in

the water with supervised mooring facilities if available.

Can be used by nonswimmers, families, guests, without fear of capsize.

Can be used for weekend cruise or entertaining without expenses of travel, lodging and meals. Has sleeping accommodation,

Can be sailed safely on large lakes or on the sea where winds and waves are generally higher.

More equipment for navigation, comforts and cooling can be carried,

Longer waterline boat has greater hull speed.

Has more protection from waves, sun and cold weather.

Often a decision is obvious to some because of cost or available mooring space or family considerations. The subject of choosing a keelboat is handled in great detail by George Harvey's book "offshore I", published by the Ontario Sailing Association. It also covers family cruising, buying, financing, old versus new, seamanship etc. Many useful tips for new owners of keelboats are included. Do not assume because four bunks are designed into a boat, four adults can live comfortably. "offshore I" by Victor Searles is a delightful, educational experience in cruising.

Which boat to buy?

If your first decision was a centreboard boat, ask yourself the following questions or consider these points:

(1) Do I want to race? If so, what class is raced locally?

(2) What size boat do I need for passengers and size of waves likely to be encountered? A sloop under 14 feet is only suitable for small waves.

(3) Do I want a one-man boat, a sloop or a catamaran?

(4) Do I want comfortable, safe, nonathletic sailing, or fast exciting sport (sometimes wet), and usually for two persons only?

(5) Consider too if you want ultra simplicity in rig and adjustments of sail shape or all the go-fast ideas built in. This can add 25% to the boat cost. For racing buy the best, or add custom adjustment devices yourself.

(6) It pays to find out more about the builder and class association of the boat you like. If the boat has only one builder, thousands of miles away, it may be difficult getting problems corrected. A strong class association can improve builder quality.

(7) Examine the workmanship, fastening of fittings, sealings around buoyancy tanks, buoyancy distribution, flexing of hull, floor, strength of bow and rudder fittings, type of mast buoyancy or draining. Some of these are difficult to improve later yourself.

(8) If you may race the boat, find out where racing fleets are located and whether the builder guarantees the boat to "measure-in". Also find out how close it is guaranteed to minimum weight.

(9) Look for places to stow clothing, pails, anchor, paddles, and whisker pole.

(10) Find out if buoyancy tanks have closed cell foam blocks inside, sealed in vinyl bags. Are there tank-drain plugs to check for leaks? Is it guaranteed to pass a buoyancy test?

(11) Does it have adequate transom flaps and automatic floor-bailers for easy self-rescue?

(11) Does it have deck and seats that are comfortable for sitting in and hiking out?

(13) Are hiking straps suitable and adjustable for different crews and helmsman to hike comfortably?

(14) Is the hiking tiller long enough for sitting forward and hiking and with swivel fitting for easy tacking and gybing?

(15) Are there adequate winch or power ratio devices for jib halyard and boomvang adjustment?

(16) Is the boat class a CYA recognized National Class with boats in many provinces.

(17) If the boat is roomy and wide enough for safe cruising, does it have buoyancy enough to prevent sinking? Is buoyancy placed to prevent turning turtle and to allow bailing out when righted. A demonstration is necessary if this is not assured; it is very important.

Choice of materials for boats

Fiberglass reinforced plastic is the most common material used in both keelboats and centreboard boats. It eliminates the old problem in planked wooden boats of caulking, soaking up rot. Fiberglass requires much less maintenance than wood and can last a long time. The workmanship of the builder is almost as important as in wood because it is usually made by hand lay-up. Technique and care control weight, strength, and joints at deck and at buoyancy tanks to prevent leaks. Most centreboard boats are available in fiberglass only.

Wood is still used in some classes. It may be a design such as the Mirror dinghy or pram suitable for kit or home construction in marine plywood. Hot, or cold moulded plywood is an excellent material because it is light, strong and often produces a stiffer hull than fiberglass. It lasts 2030 years or more with proper, construction and maintenance. When varnished, it is beautiful, but needs refinishing almost every year when exposed to much sun.

A few sailboats are built of aluminum. The Petrel class is one that is built in aluminum and used in many sailing programs because it is light, strong and stands up well to a lot of use. The construction requires rivetting which does impose some limitation on shape and finish.

Daysailing in a centreboard boat up to 24 feet long

This type of sailing must be within sight of shore, with good weather forecast and winds to suit your boat, and sailing ability. It can be quiet and relaxing or thrilling and physically demanding. Safety and self-rescue ability are of prime importance. You usually do not need a lot of equipment. Safety and comfort equipment required:

(1) PFD's for everyone aboard.

(2) Paddles, bailing buckets, compass, anchor and line, snack and refreshment when the weather is hot.

(3) Extra line, spare shackles, pliers, screwdriver and tape.

(4) Rainwear suits, extra sweater, sunscreen or suntan lotion, hat and sunglasses.

To be enjoyed, convenience of adjustments, rigging and trailering should be planned so there is more time to sail.

Cruising

These remarks apply mainly to centreboard boats up to 24 feet long and stable enough for weekend cruising within sight of land and also to small keel boats.

Enjoyable cruising is usually based on relaxed enjoyment, avoiding high winds, weather hazards and reaching port for overnight anchoring with plenty of safety factor.

The boat has to be large enough for the people and conditions expected. If you choose the wrong boat for your needs, you may be limited in where you can go safely or in the comfort and enjoyment of family or guests. Size is always a compromise for living below deck and stowing all the necessary equipment and supplies.

These factors help make cruising more enjoyable:

(1) Good planning of what to take and where to stow everything.

(2) Planning where to go and where to anchor overnight

(3) Forecast weather to avoid calm, storm or rain that might spoil the cruise.

(4) Take sufficient food that can be kept without spoiling and with minimum cooking.

(5) Avoid injury, sunburn and sea sickness.

(6) Be prepared for proper anchoring and observe cruising etiquette.

(7) Take people who enjoy cruising and make it enjoyable.

(8) Safety.

(1) Good planning, requires a check list of food, clothing, safety equipment, tools, fuel, Cooking stove should use alcohol not gasoline, coal oil or benzine for safety and odour reasons. If food needs refrigeration, take ice in well-insulated cooler, keep out of sun and wind, and further insulate in the day time with sleeping bag or equivalent. Also keep food in well insulated cooler and

avoid foods that spoil easily. Meat and milk spoil rapidly above 50° F to 150° F. Have guests bring duffle bags. Take large plastic bags to keep things dry. Do not bury safety gear, PFDs, rainwear, anchor and rode below other gear. Carry a spare anchor and spare line. Take a radio for weather warnings.

(2) Do not plan too ambitious a distance. Too long underway before anchoring is tiring. Find your anchorage spot early. Allow for poor winds or head winds to return on time. Plan to suit guests' enjoyment more than your own, they may not enjoy long passage and may get seasick if it gets rough Consider children or they may not want to go next time. If i rains, it can be crowded and miserable below deck. Small children usually cannot stand a voyage of more than two hour at a time. When they are teenagers, they may become excellent crew.

(3) The three-day weather forecast, Marine forecast and weather system approaching must be considered before leaving. Weather is often good before calm or storm. Observe all signs to confirm forecast has not changed. Call the weather information office for specific area predictions and observe the signs in the clouds to give warning in time to take proper action. It is safer and better to postpone a trip than have a risky or unpleasant cruise.

(4) Food can be simple, delicious and nutritious without much cooking. Take canned meat, fresh carrots and vegetables, cheese, nuts, cookies, fresh fruit (not soft), dates, figs and raisins, powdered milk, cocoa, tea, coffee and whole wheat bread. These foods keep easily and do not require much preparation. Take enough fresh water for drinks and to clean dishes and cutlery. Avoid any risk of food spoiling or poisoning. A full cooked

meal may be very difficult to prepare without proper stove and work space. Food poisoning causes diarrhea, vomiting and high temperature, and requires rest and no liquids.

(5) Avoid injury by inexperienced hands on sheets and winches. The power of the wind may surprise them, Be sure everyone knows location of safety equipment and man overboard procedures, especially if the skipper goes over. Do a practice run if possible. Beware of fair skin and sunburn while on the water. Use sunscreen on exposed skin to avoid painful burn and disagreeable side effects. Wear sunglasses to avoid headache from glare. Do not forget a first-aid kit.

Sea sickness can be very unpleasant, spoiling a cruise for everyone. Some things help prevent it. It can be brought on by a series of conditions such as cold and hunger, hot stale air, watching the boat roll and not having some specific task.

It is better to lie down, eyes closed, not sit down. Avoid smells of food, gasoline, and keep warm and dry, avoid too much tea or liquid. Taking seasick pills helps the mind, not the stomach, and causes drowsiness. They must be taken before the feelings of seasickness come. When on deck, watch the horizon, not the boat going up and down.

It can be a serious feeling for the one affected and they can seldom do work. Be sure they wear safety harness on deck because there is no feeling of need to survive. There is no cure except the magic of solid ground.

(6) Anchoring is fully covered in a previous chapter. On a cruise, finding a suitable spot may be the key to a happy trip. You will spend more time at anchor than

sailing, so shelter, safe protection, considerate neighbours and lack of insect nuisance are important.

There are certain accepted points of etiquette. You have no right to ask someone to move their anchor if they arrived before you. You are responsible to avoid swinging into them if the wind changes. Avoid constant banging of halyards on the mast and noise after sleeping time begins. Voices carry on smooth water incredibly far on a still night.

It may be wise to post rules that apply aboard your boat so that guests know where they stand. If you don't want smoking in the cabin, for example, it should be stated. Observe customs that apply in other clubs or harbours. If you are a member of a yacht club, you are automatically welcome to visit another. You never go aboard another boat without being invited. People who own a boat guard their privacy and there should be times for everyone when they can be on their own.

If you must dock or raft alongside other boats, have fenders ready to avoid touching hulls anywhere. Have docking lines ready and accept a sailor's assistance on the dock when offered. Do the same when on shore yourself.

Flag etiquette is simple. The Canadian flag is flown from the stern, the club burgee from the mast head. The Canadian flag should be approximately one inch long per foot of boat. In foreign waters, fly that country's flag from your starboard shroud below the spreader as a courtesy, as well as the Canadian flag from the stern.

(7) One of the most important points in enjoying cruising is compatible companions. There is no place for criticism or bad manners. In order to have a safe and proper attitude, train crew properly, choose guests carefully, consider their enjoyment first and make it clear

that the skipper must be responsible and in charge of the boat, no matter who is at the helm.

Do not assume that guests know what to do or even the sailing language to speak if they are not sailors.

Racing

Some sailors get bitten by the racing bug after their first race, even if they come in last. The challenges offered in racing are never ending. The range of competition is from club level upto international, even for husband and wife teams. Bronze Sail proficiency standards prepare you best for racing because they develop more competent abilities than those of the average person racing. Many adults, for example, start to race before they learn to sail well. By learning rules and tactics, getting some experience, you can easily go on to Silver sail level or beyond and do well in most racing circuits.

When some people see the seriousness with which many people approach racing, they think it must not be relaxing. It is relaxing, because it promotes physical and mental challenge so different from the daily routine, it completely unwinds your tensions. It has technical challenge too, depending on the class you choose. A pram and a Flying Dutchman might be two extremes, but each class has fun racing equal boats. Handicap racing is not quite the same type of boat for boat competition but is enjoyed by many.

If you plan to race, a good way to start is to crew for someone in a class you think you will like, and find out if that is the class you want to join into. Racing is also taught in many sailing schools. Club racing and regattas are fun. Your toughest competitor may be your best friend. For young people, it teaches self-reliance, concentration, sportsmanship and promotes better physical fitness.

The fundamentals, boat handling, tuning and maintenance become very important in winning, You have a regular means of testing techniques and ideas. Racing makes you a better sailor, Some people enjoy the tactics of starting, wind shifts and using the rules to advantage. One sure thing about racing seriously is that it becomes a vital part of your life and that many of your friends are sailors. Try racing, if it does not appeal to you, it is more likely that an investment in crusing is right for you.

Many Bronze sail courses include racing in their program because it is such a good way to test your improvement in ability. It certainly adds a lot of fun to a program and leads naturally to the next level, Silver Sail. If you can master the skills required in Bronze level, adding rules and tactics and a little more heavy weather practice will surely show in greatly improved racing results.

Trailering

Most dinghy sailors at one time or another, move their boats to a lake or back, some, each time they sail. This section covers the more important points about selecting the right trailer type, and what to do to make trailering easier and safer on the road. It does not deal with heavy-duty types with more than two wheels requiring brakes or sway control devices.

Most centreboard boats weigh between 125 and 700 lbs, an can be handled safely on a trailer weighing 200-300 lbs with the proper hitch and fastening to the boat. There are lots of ideas used by racing sailors, who trail often, to make things more convenient and cut down the time to pack up and get going. Through lack of experience, forgetting, or improper equipment, the following things do happen when trailing sailboats: For example, boats have been damaged slipping off rollers or tipping while loading or unloading, have come off the trailer on the highway at 60 m.p.h., had mast or boom come loose and scratch the boat or damage the aluminum, or been damaged by improper support or vibration, Sailors have had to leave their boats and trailers overnight on the highway because wheel bearings overheated or failed, because lights didn't work or tires went flat. Proper design, fastening and maintenance, and planning prior to the time you need to go will eliminate most problems. You can avoid having to find four or six strong backs to lift your boat on to the trailer at a regatta, Don't let trailering spoil your fun.

Design—for convenience

it is nice to be able to back your trailer to the water's edge, tilt up the hinged bed fitted with winch, and hook on to the bow. With a person to steady it, you should be able to wind up the cable, lock the boat in place, lower the bed, unrig and fasten boat and rigging ready to go in 15 minutes. To do this requires some planning and some prefitted wooden pieces to fit the boat. Tiedown straps, shock cord and heavy clips can hold your boat, mast and boom without danger of damage.

The trailer should have wide rubber rollers at the back to protect the boat from slipping off as it comes up. Even wringer-washer rollers can be used if the trailer you have or buy is not suitable. It should move along rollers and carpetted supports that keep it from tipping over with mast up. Supports can be lengthwise and hinged in the middle to fit, or turned across the trailer and fitted to the curve at each side.

Supports should be provided under the keel at the

mast step and under the aft end of the centreboard trunk where the hull is quite rigid. The hull should also be supported at each side near shroud points and 1/4 of the way aft near the round of the bilge. Avoid supports that tend to flex the hull and eventually cause crazing or gel coat damage, or damage to buoyancy tanks.

The hand-operated ratchet winch should be mounted high enough to meet the bow fitting where the winch hook goes. Use the strongest available dacron line of about 5/16 diameter. It can last 15 years. If wire-rope winch cable is used, you should have gloves to handle it. If the boat is only 125 lbs, two people can lift it on easily, but the key safety feature is a foolproof bolted, strong hook up at the bow and fitted into a padded Vee. Multiple boat trailers need special design.

Make a wooden padded piece to fit across the hull opposite the back of the trailer. This provides a place to hook side straps pulling down to the trailer and preventing side movement. The mast and boom can also be fitted to this to prevent them touching the boat. Shock cord with end clips is handy to retain the mast in place. In the mast step, and retained by the mast gate, use a post, shaped to take mast and boom at the right height. Let the mast overlap the car trunk lid when open. You now have the boat and rigging fastened in minutes instead of an hour and safe from damage. Put your smooth rudder in the trunk.

Tongue weight

To properly set up a trailer for the road, you need the weight located over the wheels in such a way that 5 to 10% of the total boat and trailer weight rests on the ball fitting of the car. To do this, move the boat forward until the tongue weighs say 50 lbs for an average dinghy on a bathroom scale. Adjust the winch support to that location and road test it. Sway indicates more weight is needed.

Hitch

The trailer hitch must be bolted to the frame of the car for a proper job. There must be a locking device on the fitting that locks on the ball: usually a [ever that snaps down when properly in place or a screw adjustment. The law requires proper chains as a safety device to prevent the tongue from dropping down to the road or swinging out of control. The length of each must just allow full turning.

Wheels and bearings

The one item liable to cause trouble is wheel bearings. Trailer wheels come in different sizes and standard wheel bearing kits are available in case they wear. They are roller bearings adjusted in the same way as car front wheel bearings and must be kept greased and dry. The rubber seal can wear, so backing the wheels into the water above the axle may start rust and wear and bearing failure. Carry a small scissor jack for trailer when boat is loaded. Grease bearings once a year and spin the wheel to check the sound periodically. Also feel hubs to be sure bearings run cool after highway driving. The temperature will depend on the loading also. Never back warm bearings into water, they will suck water in as they cool and may require cleaning and greasing.

Lights

Trailers require a four-wire system to hook up to car stop lights, tail lights, direction signals and licence plate light. A heavier flasher unit in the car may be required. The socket connection should be long enough to fit inside the car trunk to keep dry in rain. The main problem with lights is caused by immersing them in the water, allowing corrosion to form and cause high resistance.

Grease all sockets and bulbs, drain or completely seal lights. Never back trailer wheels or lights into salt water. Corrosion is very rapid.

Tires

Tire pressure depends on load and rating. Each tire has a maximum load rating on it. Never exceed the rating or tread will wear in the centre, the ride will be hard and they may blow out. Under-inflation will cause overheating and side-wall damage if the rated load is applied. The boat should not be subjected to unnecessary vibration or buoyancy tank seams could begin to leak after a lot of trailering. Deflate buoyancy bags each time you travel.

Driving with trailer

The first time will concern some drivers when they have to back to the water's edge. Remember you must turn the trailer tongue one way by turning the front of the car the other way then straighten out. It takes a little practice and you should be able to see the back of the trailer to see what is happening. Beware of jackknifing the trailer and damaging something. Back slowly and have someone outside guide you to be sure no one is in the way.

Always be aware on the highway that stopping takes longer. Allow 50% farther to the car ahead and keep to the curb lane if possible. Mileage is poorer especially at the speed limit. It's a good idea on each trip to check hitch and tie downs yourself. Stop after a few miles and check once more that everything in the boat is under control and not blowing away. Check the temperature of trailer wheels on a longer trip. It will give warning before damage is done to bearings or bearing races. Check lights each time before you leave. Some people who drive on gravel roads use a full cover over and under the boat to prevent gel coat or paint chipping. Others make a plywood floor for the trailer. Drive slowly on rough roads. The trailer doesn't have shock absorbers, as on a car. Spend a few hours organizing your trailering equipment for happier safer trips with the boat.

13

RULES OF THE NAVIGATION

One of the first things you will notice when you begin sailing is the traffic. America's recreational waterways are becoming more and more crowded every year. Unfortunately, along with the crowding there has been a noticeable increase in the number of accidents. Thus to enjoy sailing and to avoid accidents it becomes necessary to thoroughly master the traffic rules that govern the movements of boats. These rules are called the rules of the road; their fundamental purpose is to avoid collisions. The rules apply to all types of boats, and cover all of the possible types of meetings that can take place between two boats. In all of these instances the rules determine the boat that is *privileged* and the boat that is *burdened.* A privileged boat has the *right of way,* and is entitled to, and to a large extent is obligated to maintain course and speed. The burdened boat must look out for the privileged boat; it must alter course and/or speed so that it does not interfere with the privileged boat.

In almost all instances, a sailboat under sail alone has the right of way over a powerboat. This means that powerboats should stay clear of sailboats at all times. The important exceptions to this rule are as follows. A sailboat overtaking and passing a powerboat is burdened; it must stay clear. Another exception refers to meetings between sailboats and very large powered vessels in restricted channels. Neither sailboats nor powerboats under sixty-five feet in length can claim the right of way over large, powered vessels that can navigate only inside a restricted channel. The safest application of this rule is to attempt to stay clear of all other vessels when sailing in a narrow channel. As we mentioned earlier, this situation will probably only occur if you attempt to tack upwind in a narrow channel. It is far better to find another way to get through the channel. Finally, remember that all other vessels, including sailboats under sail alone, must stay clear of fishing vessels using nets or lines or trawls.

An informal rule that you should take to heart and employ whenever you are in doubt is as follows: *Don't press your advantage!* With the very large number of inexperienced boatmen now crowding the waterways, you cannot count on the other man knowing the rules or correctly anticipating your intentions. We repeat: If you are in doubt about the situation, make every attempt to stay clear. Such common sense and courtesy will go a long way toward making your hours on the water both happy and safe.

Rules for boats under sail alone

As you become familiar with the following rules, you will note that they favor the boat that is sailing closehauled. That is, the privileged boat is the one that is closehauled. This ruling dates back to the days of the square-riggers, vessels that sailed poorly to windward. Sailing closehauled was thus favored by the seafaring men who originally established the rules of the road.

The rules are as follows. Whenever two sailing vessels are approaching each other in such a way that there is a risk of collision, one of the vessels must stay clear. The possible situations and the rules are: (a) A *boat that is running free will stay clear of a boat that is closehauled.* The boat running free is burdened. (b) A *boat closehauled on the port tack will stay clear of a boat closehauled on the starboard tack.* The boat on the port tack is burdened. (c) *When both boats are running free, but with the wind on different sides, the boat that has the wind on the port side will stay clear of the other.* Again, the boat on the port tack is burdened. Remember it this way: port, red, danger, burdened. (d) *When both boats are running free, with the wind on the same side, the boat that is to windward will stay clear of the boat that is to leeward.* In this case, the boat that is upwind is burdened. (e) A *boat that has the wind aft will stay clear of the other vessel.*

It is very important that you learn these rules well and that you apply them. At the same time keep in mind that many boatmen will not know the rules and that you will be forced to assume the responsibility for preventing accidents. By all means be upset when you observe failure to abide by the rules of the road. And you will observe such failure. We can only say that education is the answer to this type of problem. You may find yourself in a position someday to help by participating in either the U.S. Power Squadron or Coast Guard Auxiliary safe-boating programs. We hope that you will respond when the opportunity presents itself. Also keep in mind that the rules given above do *not apply* to sailboats in a race. The racing rules differ somewhat from the rules above, and apply only to the boats in the race; they do not apply to boats that happen onto a racing course.

Rules for boats under power

Many small sailboats use outboard engines as auxiliary power. Whenever your sailboat is being powered by an engine-even if the sails are up—the boat is a motorboat according to the law and must follow the motorboat rules of the road. These rules differ from the sailing rules. They are as follows: (a) Two *motorboats approaching each other head on should pass port side to port side.* When the skipper of one of the boats alters course to starboard to honor this rule, he should give one short blast on his born. The other skipper should then acknowledge by returning the single short blast. In the event two boats are approaching each other and will pass starboard to starboard, two short blasts on the horn should be given to indicate that course is being altered to port. Wherever possible, the boats should pass port side to port side, although instances do occur when it is more practical to pass starboard side to starboard side. (b) A *motorboat having another boat in its danger zone (from dead ahead to two points abaft the starboard beam) must stay clear.* The drawing shows how the "danger zone" rule applies. It may even be necessary to stop or reverse direction to stay clear. (c) Any *boat leaving a slip, or a berth at a dock, has* no *rights until it is entirely clear.* This means that the boat leaving the slip or dock must consider itself burdened until it is completely clear of the dock and in open water.

Additional horn signals you should learn to recognize are (a) three short blasts—my boat is proceeding astern, and (b) four or more blasts—danger!

Lights

There isn't room, nor is there any need, to discuss in detail here the regulations covering the lights required on different types of vessels. As a small-boat sailor, you will probably sail at night only very rarely. If your boat is not equipped with running lights of any kind, there are just two things you should keep in mind. First, remember that the starboard running light is green, and that the port running light is red. With this in mind, you can usually identify the course another boat is sailing at night. Second, should it be necessary for you to sail at night, have a flashlight or lantern available. Then, at the approach of another boat, you should flash the light on your sails to indicate your position and approximate course and speed. If you intend to sail extensively at night, of course, full navigation lights will be required. In addition, you will have to learn the various light combinations used on other vessels. All of this information is contained in various Coast Guard pamphlets. These are free of charge from any Coast Guard office.

We shall briefly discuss three important *aids to navigation* in this chapter. These are *charts,* the *system of buoys* used on United States waters, and the *compass.* These three tools are indispensable to the sailor, especially the small-boat sailor who spends virtually all of his time on the waters near the shoreline. It is important to note that although charts, buoys, and the compass are called aids to navigation, their use in coastwise sailing is called *piloting. To* be more exact, piloting is close-to-shore navigation that uses visible landmarks, sound signals, and soundings. The visible landmarks the sailor uses include buoys, light signals, and distinctive structures on land. For example, once a sailor becomes familiar with his home waters, be will know where be is at any time by recognizing such structures as church steeples, water tanks, smokestacks, and unusual buildings. The sound signals all sailors become familiar with include bell, gong, and whistle buoys, and horns installed on lighthouses. A sounding is a measurement of the depth of the water. Soundings are taken to make sure there is enough water to keep the boat afloat, but also to help determine position, When a series of soundings is matched to a chart, it gives a rough approximation of position.

Charts

A chart is a nautical "road map." It is easily the most important aid to navigation available to the sailor. With a chart, be can determine where be is and what the waters hold. Without one, he might as well be blind, for he has no clue to what lies below the surface of the water. Charts of the coastal waters of the United States are published by the U.S. Coast and Geodetic Survey and distributed by the Coast Guard. Charts of the Great Lakes and the Mississippi River are produced by the U. S. Army Corps of Engineers.

The illustration shows a small portion of a typical chart. There isn't room here to describe everything shown on charts, but we can point out a few of the more important features. The numbers shown offshore in various positions indicate the depth of the water at mean low tide. The diamond-shaped symbols next to small dots represent buoys. The solid, heavy dots represent navigational lights. For example, the lighted buoy just east of the southern tip of Deer Island is a flashing red (FL R) light. There's a good deal more to charts than this very brief introduction, When you begin sailing, you should make it a point to become thoroughly familiar with the charts covering the waters you plan to use. You wouldn't think of making a long auto trip through strange country without a road map. Be just as sensible about sailing, and always have and use the chart covering the waters you are cruising,

Another very important feature of all charts is the *compass rose.* As the drawing shows, the compass rose consists of two circles, each calibrated into 360 degrees. The outer circle indicates *true north,* while the inner circle shows the direction of *magnetic north.* At the center of the compass rose the *variation is* shown, as well as how much it changes annually. Variation is simply the difference between true north and magnetic north for a given area.

It's important to understand the difference between true north and magnetic north, for the compass on your boat points to magnetic north, not true north. Of course, if there are some objects containing iron near the boat's compass, its reading will be affected. This effect is called *deviation.* Correcting for deviation is important for pinpoint navigation, but it need not concern you if you make sure no tools, machinery, or a radio are stored near the compass. In practice, the sailor looks at the magnetic circle of the compass rose to determine the course he must sail to reach a given destination, and then steers accordingly, using the boat's compass.

There is, of course, a great deal more to the use of charts than we have described here. Mastering the use of a chart is a task requiring much study and attention to detail. It is worth the effort, however, for someday a quick and accurate reading of a chart may save you from running onto a pile of rocks or aground on a sandbar.

Buoys

In general, two types of buoys are in use on U.S. waters: unlighted buoys without sounds, and buoys that have sound and/or light. Buoys are used in a systematic way that makes it very clear to a sailor where he should steer his boat. This system is based on color, buoy shape, and numbering.

Imagine you are entering a channel or harbor from seaward. As you proceed up the channel, you will note that the buoys on the right-hand side are red; they are also marked with even numbers. The use of *red* for buoys on the *right* of a channel has given rise to a simple memory device: think *Red, Right, Returning* and you will always remember to leave the red buoys to starboard as you enter a channel, harbor, or river from seaward. Of course, when you are going toward the sea you would leave the red buoys to port.

The left-band side of a channel is marked by black buoys with odd numbers. Buoy shape also distinguishes the right from the left side of a channel. The red buoys on the right are conical in shape; they are called *nun* buoys. The black buoys on the left are cylindrical; they are called can buoys. Two other color schemes are in use. In one, black and white vertical stripes on an unnumbered buoy mark the middle of a channel. Boats should pass close by, but on either side of this type of buoy. In the other color scheme, black and red horizontal bands on a buoy indicate a channel junction or some type of underwater obstruction inside the channel itself. These buoys should be given a wide berth. They may be passed on either side, but the color of the top band indicates the preferred channel. In the drawing, for example, the red and black junction buoy's top band is red. Thus the preferred channel is to the left of the buoy; the boat leaves the red top to its starboard.

Buoys that have special importance to the navigator are lighted, equipped with sound, or both. Such buoys mark the entrance to a harbor; they are also used to mark a bend in a channel. To get some idea of the importance of light and sound in buoys, just consider the following situations. You are sailing on open water at night, and want to enter a sheltered harbor. As you approach land its mass is solid black to the eye. No landmarks are discernible. The entrance to the harbor, however, is marked by two lighted buoys. The one an the right will have either a red or a white light, with regular or quick flashing. The buoy on the left will have either a green or white light, again with regular or quick flashing. Your chart will tell you the color of the lights and also the nature of the flashing. Your job is to spot the buoys, and then sail cautiously between them to enter the harbor.

In the second situation, suppose you are caught in fog, but know the general direction toward a sheltered harbor you wish to enter. Reference to your chart will tell you immediately if the harbor entrance is marked by bell or whistle buoys. With this information, you should proceed very cautiously toward the harbor entrance, following the sound of the buoys. Go very slowly and with great care in fog. You must be alert constantly to the possibility of collision. In addition, because sound behaves very strangely in fog, you must be alert to the possibility of straying away from the center of the harbor entrance.

One final comment about buoys is necessary. Every effort is made to maintain buoys in good condition and in their proper positions. This does not mean, however, that they will always be correctly placed. They may be adrift, off their charted positions due to heavy storms, unusual tides, and collisions, or even missing entirely. Because of these possibilities, a reasonable distance should always be allowed between the boat and a buoy when the buoy is passed.

The compass

If your sailing will never take you out of sight of familiar landmarks, you can probably do without a compass. On the other hand, if you plan to sail on large lakes, bays, or sounds, a good compass is a must. The compass should be mounted securely for easy reading by the helmsman, and away from large, iron-containing objects and electrical equipment. Always check before going out to make sure no iron or steel objects are near the compass. More than once I have discovered a sack of tools near the compass. The tools were placed there temporarily, but then forgotten. The deviation produced by such objects can greatly affect the compass reading.

Each compass has a line on its outside ring called the *lubberline.* This line indicates the heading of the boat; thus the compass must be mounted so that the lubberline and the centerline of the boat are parallel or coincide. When the compass has been installed in this position, the helmsman knows that the boat is beaded in exactly the same direction as the compass reads. Of course, as you recall, this is the magnetic course, not the true course, which is represented by the outer ring of the compass rose.

If you are really interested in mastering the art of coastwise piloting, several other aids to navigation become necessary. These include (a) *dividers,* for measuring distance on the chart; (b) *parallel rules,* for plotting and moving a course on a chart to the nearest compass rose; (c) a *lead line,* a weighted line used to measure the depth of the water; (d) *Coast Pilots,* books that give complete descriptions of ports, harbors, and coastlines; (e) *tide and current tables and charts,* and *M light and buoy lists.* Finally, a small *radio direction finder* (RDF) is a must if you expect to sail out of sight of land. An RDF allows you to get radio bearings—that is, the direction of a radio beacon or standard broadcast station from the boat. If you know the location on a chart of two or more sending stations, getting these bearings permits you to plot your position. An RDF is an indispensable aid in fog.

INDEX